RAVEL REMEMBERED

Roger Nichols is a writer and broadcaster, specializing in French music of the nineteenth and twentieth centuries. He is the author of *Debussy Remembered* and *Mendelssohn Remembered*, as well as *Conversations with Madeleine Milhaud*, all published by Faber.

Ravel
Remembered

ROGER NICHOLS

faber and faber
LONDON · BOSTON

First published in 1987
by Faber and Faber Limited
3 Queen Square London wc1n 3au

Photoset by Goodfellow & Egan, Cambridge
Printed in England by Clays Ltd, St Ives plc

A CIP record for this book
is available from the British Library

isbn 0–571–14986–3

2 4 6 8 10 9 7 5 3 1

Contents

List of illustrations

Introduction

An image survives in some quarters of Ravel as a cold-hearted, cynical, self-absorbed person who had no life outside his work and who even in that sphere existed only by proxy, as it were, living parasitically off established aesthetic and formal models, never venturing beyond the safe enclosures of the sonata and the minuet. This volume does not specifically address the image of Ravel's music, although a certain amount of anecdotal evidence naturally accrues along the way. But the above image of Ravel the man needs rectifying, all the more so because in certain circumstances it was true. If you were a pushy admirer, an inquisitive critic or a brainless virtuoso, then you did best to stay away from him: his coldness towards such people could be truly glacial. For his friends, though, he found no trouble too great, no kindness too extravagant, and what Tristan Klingsor called 'the ironic and tender heart that beats under the velvet jacket of Maurice Ravel' is amply attested in the memoirs that follow.

Inevitably, most of these memoirs come from musicians – fellow composers like Stravinsky, Milhaud, Poulenc and Vaughan Williams, as well as singers, pianists and conductors. But even if Ravel had many musician friends, their conversations were by no means always about music. Ravel was also interested in politics, philosophy, gardening, cooking, cats, walking, swimming, looking at nature and collecting preposterous bits of bric-à-brac. When on form (and not worried by some problem in a current composition) he was a delightful companion. Unfortunately we cannot now recapture his considerable gifts as a storyteller and mimic, though readers may be glad to be spared the long walks through Paris in the small hours which were often the price that had to be paid for such delights.

There are, of course, lacunae among the 'witnesses' which it would have been a pleasure to see filled: we have nothing (or at least nothing worth repeating) from Ansermet, Auric, Dukas, Ibert, Saint-Saëns or Satie. The opinions of the last would no doubt have been particularly stimulating, to judge by acid little comments he did let drop, like: 'M. Ravel refuses the Legion of Honour, but all his music accepts it'. I have dealt with lacunae of another sort – passages omitted as being irrelevant or uninteresting – simply by passing over their removal in the text itself, as I feel that rows of dots interrupt the flow of the narrative. But sources at the end of each extract are quoted exactly. Where no translation of a French source is acknowledged, the translation is mine. Nearly three-quarters of the extracts are here appearing in English for the first time.

Docklow   ROGER NICHOLS
Herefordshire   April 1987

Acknowledgements

I am grateful for permission to quote from the following copyright material (detailed source references are given at the end of each extract):

Théophile Alajouanine, 'Aphasia and Artistic Realization', *Brain*; Louis Aubert, Jacques-Emile Blanche, Jean Cocteau, E. J. Dent, Marcelle Gerar, Mimi Godebska (Mme Godebska-Blacque-Belair), Nils Grevillius, Valentine Hugo, Désiré-Emile Inghelbrecht, Hélène Jourdan-Morhange, Marguerite Long, Joaquín Nin, Charles Oulmont, Henri Sauguet, Paul Stefan, André Suarès, Ricardo Viñes, Emile Vuillermoz, *La Revue Musicale (ReM)*; Jane Bathori, 'Les Musiciens que j'ai connus', tr. Felix Aprahamian, *Recorded Sound* (British Library National Sound Archive); Alexandre Benois, *Reminiscences of the Russian Ballet* (Putnam, 1941); André Beucler, *Poet of Paris, Twenty Years with Léon-Paul Fargue* (Chatto & Windus, 1955); M. D. Calvocoressi, *Musician's Gallery* (Faber & Faber, 1933); Alfredo Casella, Frank Martin, 'Speculum', *Musical Times*; René Chalupt, *Ravel au miroir de ses lettres* (Robert Laffont, 1956); Colette, Léon-Paul Fargue, Tristan Klingsor, Roland-Manuel, Emile Vuillermoz, *Maurice Ravel par quelques-uns de ses familiers* (Editions du Tambourinaire, 1939); Piero Coppola, *Dix-sept ans de musique à Paris, 1922–1939* (Editions Slatkine, 1982); Maurice Delage (Bibliothèque Nationale); Norman Demuth, *Ravel* (Dent, 1947); Manuel de Falla, *On Music and Musicians* (Marion Boyars, 1979); Léon-Paul Fargue, *Maurice Ravel* (Domat, 1949); Henriette Faure, *Mon maître Maurice Ravel* (Editions ATP, 1978); Mikhail Fokine, *Memoirs of a Ballet Master* (Constable, 1961); Arthur Honegger, *Incantation aux fossiles* (Editions d'Ouchy, 1948); Hélène Jourdan-Morhange, *Ravel et nous* (Editions du Milieu du Monde, 1945); Hélène Jourdan-Morhange and Vlado Perlemuter, *Ravel d'après Ravel* (Editions du Cervin, 1957); Marguerite Long, *At the Piano with Ravel* (Dent, 1973); Alma Mahler Werfel, *And the Bridge is Love* (Harcourt Brace Jovanovich Inc., 1959); Edmond Maurat, *Souvenirs musicaux et littéraires* (Université de Saint-Etienne, 1977); Darius Milhaud (BBC); Francis Poulenc, *Moi et mes Amis* (La Palatine, 1963); Jules Renard, *Journal* (La Bibliothèque de la Pléiade, *Journal* 1887–1910 ed. Guichard & Sigaux,

© Edition Gallimard, 1960); Roland-Manuel, *Maurice Ravel* (Dobson, 1947); Manuel Rosenthal (Radio France); Igor Stravinsky and Robert Craft, *Conversations with Igor Stravinsky* (Faber & Faber, 1959); Ursula Vaughan Williams, *RVW: a Biography,* (Oxford University Press, 1964); Ricardo Viñes, 'Journal inédit', *Revue internationale de musique française (RIMF;* Editions Slatkine); Sir Henry Wood, *My Life of Music* (Gollancz, 1938).

For permission to reproduce illustrations I am grateful to the BBC Hulton Picture Library (7, 16, 18, 22, 25), Bibliothèque Nationale (6, 20, 29, 35, 37), Michael de Cossart (11), Mlle Gaudin (36), M. Leon Leyritz (31, 32; photos, Jean Collas), Mander and Mitchenson (15), Arbie Orenstein (5), Photo Goldner (4), Photo Harlingue-Viollet (14), Photo Lipnitzki-Viollet (9, 10, 21, 24, 26), *La Revue musicale* (30), Roger-Viollet (23, 27), Roland-Manuel (3), Royal College of Music (17), Mme Alexandre Taverne (1) and M. Ariel Temporal (28; photo, Roger Roche).

Every effort has been made to contact the copyright holders of material reproduced in this book, but in some cases without success. The publishers will be pleased to hear from anyone I have not acknowledged above.

Note

Since a large number of extracts come from *La Revue musicale* this has been abbreviated as *ReM* in the source details given at the end of each piece.

Chronology

CHRONOLOGY OF RAVEL'S LIFE AND WORKS

1875 7 Mar.   Joseph Maurice Ravel born at Ciboure near Saint-Jean-de-Luz
      June   Family moves to Paris

1878   Birth of brother Edouard

FIGURES AND EVENTS IN THE ARTS

1875 Rilke, Robert Frost, Thomas Mann, Roger-Ducasse, Hahn born
      Bizet (37), Corot (79), Sterndale Bennett (59) die
      First performances: *Carmen* (Bizet), *Symphonie espagnole*
         (Lalo), Piano Concerto no. 4 (Saint-Saëns)

1876 Casals, Falla, Monteux, Vlaminck born
      First performances: *The Ring of the Nibelungs* (Wagner), *Sylvia*
         (Delibes), *La Gioconda* (Ponchielli), *The Kiss* (Smetana), *Peer Gynt*
         (Grieg's music to Ibsen's play), Symphony no. 1 (Brahms)
      Purcell Society founded

1877 Dohnányi, Cortot, Dufy, van Dongen born
      First performances: *L'Etoile* (Chabrier), *Samson et Dalila*
         (Saint-Saëns), Symphony no. 2 (Brahms), Symphony
         no. 2 (Borodin)

1878 Schreker, Masefield, Augustus John, Caplet born

1879 Beecham, Bridge, Delage, E. M. Forster, Ireland, Klee, Respighi born
      Viollet-le-Duc (65) dies
      First performances: *Eugene Onegin* (Tchaikovsky), *Une Education
         manquée* (Chabrier)

CONTEMPORARY EVENTS

1875 Third Republic founded in France
      Disraeli wins control of Suez Canal for Britain

1876 End of the Second Carlist War in Spain
      Alexander Graham Bell patents the telephone

1877 Queen Victoria proclaimed Empress of India
      Russia declares war on the Turks
      Edison invents the phonograph

1878 Paris International Exhibition
      Bulgaria established as separate principality under Turkey

1879 Jules Grévy elected President of the French Republic

RAVEL'S LIFE AND WORKS

1882 May   Begins piano lessons with Henry Ghys

FIGURES AND EVENTS IN THE ARTS

1880 Bloch, Derain, Epstein, Medtner, Pizzetti, Thibaud born
     George Eliot (61), Flaubert (59), Offenbach (61), Wieniawski (45) die
     First performances: *A May Night* (Rimsky-Korsakov), *Pirates of
     Penzance* (Sullivan)

1881 Bartók, Enescu, Léger, Miaskovsky, Picasso born
     Carlyle (86), Dostoievsky (60), Mussorgsky (42), Vieuxtemps (61) die
     First performances: *Tales of Hoffmann* (Offenbach), Piano Concerto
     no. 2 (Brahms)

1882 Braque, Joyce, Kodály, Malipiero, Stravinsky, Szymanowski,
     Virginia Woolf born
     First performance: *The Snow Maiden* (Rimsky-Korsakov)

1883 Ansermet, Bax, Casella, Kafka, Webern born
     Manet (51), Wagner (70) die
     First performance: *Lakmé* (Delibes)

1884 Modigliani born
     Smetana (60) dies
     First performances: *Manon* (Massenet), *Le Villi* (Puccini)

1885 Berg, Klemperer, D. H. Lawrence, Pound, Varèse, Wellesz born
     Victor Hugo (83) dies
     First performances: Symphony no. 7 (Bruckner), *The Mikado*
     (Sullivan)

CONTEMPORARY EVENTS

1880 Gladstone becomes Prime Minister for the second time

1881 Boers defeat British at Majuba Hill
     First Irish Home Rule Bill
     In Egypt the Mahdi announces his aim of world domination
     Canadian Pacific Railway formed
     First electric tram runs in Berlin

1882 Britain fighting in Egypt; Cairo occupied

1884 Fabian Society founded
     Invention of Maxim machine-gun

1885 Khartoum captured: General Gordon killed
     Canadian Pacific Railway completed

RAVEL'S LIFE AND WORKS

1886   Studies harmony with Charles René

1888   Meets Ricardo Viñes (12)

1889   Hears Russian and Eastern music at the 3rd Paris
                   International Exhibition
        Nov.   Enters Anthiôme's preparatory piano class at Paris
                   Conservatoire

1890 July   Wins second prize in Anthiôme's class

FIGURES AND EVENTS IN THE ARTS

1886   Alain-Fournier born
          Liszt (75) dies
          First performances: *Khovanshchina* (Mussorgsky), *Variations
          symphoniques* (Franck)

1887   Rupert Brooke, Chagall, Le Corbusier, Artur Rubinstein, Edith
          Sitwell, Villa-Lobos born
          Borodin (53) dies
          First performance: *Otello* (Verdi)

1888   Durey, Eliot, T. E. Lawrence born
          Alkan (75) dies
          First performances: *The Yeomen of the Guard* (Sullivan),
          Symphony no. 5 (Tchaikovsky)

1889   Chaplin, Cocteau born
          Gerard Manley Hopkins (45) dies
          First performance: *Don Juan* (R. Strauss)

1890   Ibert, Frank Martin, Martinů, Nijinsky, Pasternak born
          Van Gogh (37), César Franck (68) die
          First performances: *Prince Igor* (Borodin), *Cavalleria rusticana*
          (Mascagni), *The Queen of Spades* (Tchaikovsky)
          Frazer begins to publish *The Golden Bough*

CONTEMPORARY EVENTS

1886   Daimler produces his first motor car

1887   Queen Victoria's Jubilee

1888   Pasteur Institute established in Paris

1889   Paris International Exhibition: Eiffel Tower completed
          Death of Crown Prince Rudolf of Austria at Mayerling near Vienna

1890   Parnell's divorce scandal splits Irish Nationalists
          Charles de Gaulle born

RAVEL'S LIFE AND WORKS

1891 July   Wins first prize in Anthiôme's class
      Nov.   Enters piano class of de Bériot (58) and harmony class of
                Pessard (48)

1893 Feb.   With Viñes, plays Chabrier's *Trois valses romantique* to the
                composer
                Sérénade grotesque, Ballade de la Reine morte d'aimer

1895   *Un grand sommeil noir*, 'Habanera', *Menuet antique*
      July   Leaves Conservatoire

FIGURES AND EVENTS IN THE ARTS

1891 Bliss, Ernst, Prokofiev born
      Delibes (55), Seurat (32) die
      Hardy's *Tess of the D'Urbervilles* published

1892 Honegger, Milhaud born
      Lalo (69) dies
      First performances: *Pagliacci* (Leoncavallo), *Werther* (Massenet)

1893 Mayakovsky, Wilfred Owen born
      Gounod (75), Tchaikovsky (53), Maupassant (43) die
      First performances: *Hänsel und Gretel* (Humperdinck), *Manon
        Lescaut* (Puccini), *Falstaff* (Verdi), Symphony no. 6 (Tchaikovsky)

1894 E. E. Cummings, Aldous Huxley, Piston, James Thurber born
      Chabrier (53) dies
      First performances: Symphony no. 1 (Mahler), *Thaïs* (Massenet)

1895 Eluard, Robert Graves, Hindemith born
      Promenade Concerts inaugurated in London by Henry Wood
      Oscar Wilde sent to prison
      First performance: *Till Eulenspiegel* (R. Strauss)

CONTEMPORARY EVENTS

1893 Foundation of Independent Labour Party in Britain

1894 Dreyfus convicted of treason

1895 First commercial showing of moving pictures by Lumière brothers
      Freud publishes his first work on psychoanalysis
      Röntgen discovers X-rays
      Gillette invents the safety razor

RAVEL'S LIFE AND WORKS

1896   *Sainte*, 'D'Anne jouant de l'espinette'

1897   Early sonata for violin and piano. 'Entre cloches' completed
     to form with 'Habanera' the suite *Sites auriculaires*

1898 Jan. Resumes studies at Conservatoire, entering composition
     class of Fauré (53). Studies privately with Gedalge (42)
     Chanson du rouet, Si morne!, overture *Shéhérazade*
  Mar. First performance of *Sites auriculaires*
  Apr. First performance of *Menuet antique*

1899   *Pavane pour une Infante défunte*, 'D'Anne qui me jecta de la
     neige' (second of two Marot settings)
  May First performance of overture *Shéhérazade*

FIGURES AND EVENTS IN THE ARTS

1896 Gerhard, Massine, Scott Fitzgerald, Sessions born
   Bruckner (72) dies
   First performances: *Andrea Chenier* (Giordano), *La Bohème*
    (Puccini), *Der Corregidor* (Wolf)

1897 William Faulkner, Thornton Wilder born
   Brahms (64) dies

1898 Brecht, Eisenstein, Gershwin, Hemingway, Henry Moore born
   Aubrey Beardsley (26) dies
   Ballad of Reading Gaol (Wilde) published
   First performances: *Véronique* (Messager), *Sadko* (Rimsky-Korsakov)

1899 Auric, Noël Coward, Alfred Hitchcock, Lorca, Vladimir Nabokov,
    Poulenc born
   Chausson (44), Johann Strauss (74) die
   First performances: *The Tsar's Bride* (Rimsky-Korsakov), Enigma
    Variations (Elgar)

CONTEMPORARY EVENTS

1896 French annexe Madagascar

1897 Queen Victoria's Diamond Jubilee

1898 The Curies discover radium
   Zeppelin invents rigid airship

1899 Boer War
   Aspirin first marketed
   Dreyfus retried and again convicted

RAVEL'S LIFE AND WORKS

1900 Jan.   First performance of *Deux epigrammes de Clément Marot*
     May   Enters Prix de Rome competition for first time
     July   Dismissed from Fauré's class

1901 Jan.   Returns to Fauré's class as 'auditeur'
     June   Wins third prize in Prix de Rome
     Nov.   *Jeux d'eau*

1902   Fails in Prix de Rome
            Arranges vocal score of Delius's *Margot le rouge*
            Begins String Quartet

1903   Fourth failure in Prix de Rome
            Finishes String Quartet, *Manteau de fleurs*, song cycle
               Shéhérazade
            Begins *Sonatine*

FIGURES AND EVENTS IN THE ARTS

1900 Antheil, Copland, Křenek, Kurt Weill born
     Sullivan (58) dies
     First performances: *Louise* (Charpentier), *Tosca* (Puccini), *The Tale
        of Tsar Saltan* (Rimsky-Korsakov), *The Dream of Gerontius* (Elgar)

1901 Giacometti, Malraux, Rubbra, Sauguet born
     Verdi (88), Toulouse-Lautrec (37) die
     First performances: *Rusalka* (Dvořák), *Feuersnot* (R. Strauss),
        Piano Concerto no. 2 (Rachmaninov), Symphony no. 4 (Mahler)

1902 Marlene Dietrich, Ogden Nash, Walton born
     Samuel Butler (67) dies
     First performances: *Adriana Lecouvreur* (Cilea), *Pelléas et Mélisande*
        (Debussy), *Merrie England* (Edward German), Symphony no. 2
        (Sibelius)

1903 Blacher, Khachaturian, Nicholas Nabokov, Simenon, Waugh born
     Gauguin (55), Hugo Wolf (43) die
     First performance: *The Apostles* (Elgar)

CONTEMPORARY EVENTS

1900 Opening of Paris Métro
     Boer War: relief of Kimberley and of Mafeking
     Boxer Rebellion in China
     Publication of Freud's *The Interpretation of Dreams*

1901 Death of Queen Victoria
     Marconi transmits radio signals across the Atlantic
     Nobel prizes inaugurated

1902 End of Boer War

1903 First controlled flight in heavier-than-air machine by
        Wright brothers

RAVEL'S LIFE AND WORKS

1904 Mar.   First performance of String Quartet
     May   First performance of *Shéhérazade*
             Begins *Cinq mélodies populaires grecques*
     June   Meets the Godebskis

1905   Disqualified after preliminary round of Prix de Rome
     May   'L'Affaire Ravel'
             Completes *Sonatine, Introduction and Allegro, Miroirs*
             Signs contract giving M. Durand right of first refusal
                 to his works

1906 Jan.   First performance of *Miroirs*
     Mar.   First performances of *Sonatine* and *Noël des jouets*
             Begins work on *La Cloche engloutie, Histoires naturelles*

1907 Jan.   First performance of *Histoires naturelles*
     Feb.   First performance of *Introduction and Allegro*
             Vocalise-étude, Les Grands vents venus d'outre-mer,
                 Sur l'herbe
             Completes vocal score of *L'Heure espagnole*, begins
                 Rapsodie espagnole
             Gives lessons to Vaughan Williams (35)

FIGURES AND EVENTS IN THE ARTS

1904   Balanchine, Dalí, Dallapiccola, Graham Greene,
                 Kabalevsky, Skalkottas born
             Chekhov (44), Dvořák (63) die
             First performance: *Madama Butterfly* (Puccini)

1905   Greta Garbo, Jolivet, Koestler, Constant Lambert,
                 Sartre, Rawsthorne, Tippett born
             First performances: *The Merry Widow* (Lehár),
                 Salome (R. Strauss), *La Mer* (Debussy)

1906   Samuel Beckett, Betjeman, Shostakovich born
             Arensky (44), Cézanne (67), Ibsen (78) die
             First performance: *The Kingdom* (Elgar)

1907   Auden, Moravia born
             Grieg (64) dies
             First performances: *A Village Romeo and Juliet*
                 (Delius), *Ariane et Barbe-bleue* (Dukas)
             Picasso paints *Les Demoiselles d'Avignon*

CONTEMPORARY EVENTS

1904   Russo-Japanese War (1904–5)
             Entente Cordiale between France and Britain

1905   Law of Separation of Church and State passed in France
             Einstein publishes his *Special Theory of Relativity*
             Revolution in Russia

1906   San Francisco earthquake

1907   Publication of Bergson's *Creative Evolution*

RAVEL'S LIFE AND WORKS

1908 Mar.   First performance of *Rapsodie espagnole*
               Begins *Ma Mère l'Oye, Gaspard de la nuit*
      Oct.   Father dies

1909 Jan.   First performance of *Gaspard de la nuit*
      Apr.   First foreign concert, London
               Menuet sur le nom d'Haydn, Tripatos
               Orchestrates *L'Heure espagnole*
               Begins *Daphnis et Chloé*

1910 Apr.   First performance of *Ma Mère l'Oye* at inaugural
                  concert of Société musicale indépendante
      Dec.   First performance of *Chansons populaires*
               Orchestrates *Pavane pour une Infante défunte*
               Completes first version of *Daphnis* in piano score

1911 Jan.   Concerts in England and Scotland
      May   Anonymous performance of *Valses nobles et
                  sentimentales*
      19 May   Première of *L'Heure espagnole* at the Opéra-Comique,
                  Paris

FIGURES AND EVENTS IN THE ARTS

1908 Elliott Carter, Messiaen born
      Rimsky-Korsakov (64) dies
      First performances: Symphony no. 1 (Elgar), Symphony no. 7
         (Mahler)
1909 Proust begins *A la recherche du temps perdu*
      First performances: *The Golden Cockerel* (Rimsky-Korsakov),
         Elektra (R. Strauss), *Il segreto di Susanna* (Wolf-Ferrari),
         Piano Concerto no. 3 (Rachmaninov)
1910 Anouilh, Samuel Barber, Jean Genet born
      Balakirev (74), Tolstoy (82) die
      First performances: *La fanciulla del West* (Puccini),
         The Firebird (Stravinsky), Violin Concerto (Elgar), *A Sea
         Symphony* and *Fantasia on a Theme by Tallis* (Vaughan
         Williams)

1911 Mahler (51) dies
      Bruno Walter conducts posthumous first performance
         of *Das Lied von der Erde* in Vienna
      First performances: *Der Rosenkavalier* (R. Strauss),
         Petrushka (Stravinsky), Symphony no. 2 (Elgar)

CONTEMPORARY EVENTS

1909 Joan of Arc beatified
      Blériot flies across the English Channel
      Bakelite invented

1910 Union of South Africa

1911 Nationalist Republic set up in China under Sun Yat-sen
      Vitamins classified
      Amundsen reaches South Pole

RAVEL'S LIFE AND WORKS

1915 Jan.   First performance of Piano Trio. Edits Mendelssohn's
               piano music
      Feb.   Completes *Trois chansons*
      Mar.   Enlists as truck driver

1916 Sept.   Operation for dysentery. Returns to Paris to convalesce

1917 Jan.   Mother dies
      Nov.   Completes *Le Tombeau de Couperin*

1918   Orchestrates 'Alborada del gracioso' and Chabrier's
               Menuet pompeux.
               Frontispice

FIGURES AND EVENTS IN THE ARTS

1915 Saul Bellow, Arthur Miller, Orson Welles born
      Rupert Brooke (28), Scriabin (43) die
      Chaplin's film *The Tramp*

1916 Babbitt born
      Granados (49), Henry James (73), Reger (43) die
      First performance: *Savitri* (Holst)

1917 Robert Lowell, Sidney Nolan born
      Degas (83) dies
      First performances: *Turandot* (Busoni), *Arlecchino*
        (Busoni), *Palestrina* (Pfitzner), *La rondine*
        (Puccini), *Parade* (Satie)

1918 Apollinaire (38), Debussy (55), Klimt (56), Wilfred
        Owen (25), Parry (70) die
      First performances: *The Miraculous Mandarin* (Bartók),
        Il trittico (Puccini), *L'Histoire du soldat* (Stravinsky),
        Classical Symphony (Prokofiev)

CONTEMPORARY EVENTS

1915 Henry Ford develops the first farm tractor
      Einstein publishes his *General Theory of Relativity*
      'Lusitania' sunk

1916 Battles of Verdun, the Somme, Jutland

1917 Bolshevik Revolution in Russia

1918 End of First World War
      Publication of Spengler's *The Decline of the West*

RAVEL'S LIFE AND WORKS

1919 Jan.–Feb. Holiday at Mégève
     Apr.   First performance of *Le Tombeau de Couperin*
     June   Orchestrates four movements of it

1920 Jan.   Holiday at Lapras; finishes piano score of *La Valse*;
                refuses Legion of Honour
     Apr.   First performance of orchestral version of *Deux
                mélodies hébraïques*
                Begins Sonata for violin and cello; *L'Enfant et les
                sortilèges*
     Oct.   Concert in Vienna
     Nov.   *Le Tombeau de Couperin* performed as a ballet
     Dec.   First performance of *La Valse*

1921 May   Moves into 'Le Belvédère'

1922 Feb.   Completes Sonata for violin and cello (first performed April)
                Berceuse sur le nom de Gabriel Fauré
                Orchestrates Debussy's 'Sarabande' (*Pour le piano*)
                and *Danse*
                Concerts in England, Holland, Italy

FIGURES AND EVENTS IN THE ARTS

1919 Renoir (78) dies
     First performances: *Fennimore and Gerda* (Delius),
        Cello Concerto (Elgar), Symphony no. 5 (Sibelius)

1920 Maderna born
     Bruch (70), Modigliani (36) die
     First performances: *Mr Brouček's Adventures* (Janáček),
        Pulcinella (Stravinsky), *The Planets* (Holst)

1921 Saint-Saëns (86) dies
     First performances: *Le Roi David* (Honegger), *Katya
        Kabanova* (Janáček), *The Love of Three Oranges* and
        Piano Concerto no. 3 (Prokofiev)

1922 Kingsley Amis, Philip Larkin, Xenakis born
     Proust (51) dies
     James Joyce's *Ulysses*, T. S. Eliot's *The Waste Land*
        published
     First performances: *Mavra* and *Renard* (Stravinsky)

CONTEMPORARY EVENTS

1919 Treaty of Versailles
     Alcock and Brown make first transatlantic flight

1920 First meeting of League of Nations
     Prohibition of manufacture and sale of alcoholic beverages in USA

1922 BBC formed

RAVEL'S LIFE AND WORKS

1923   Begins Sonata for violin and piano
              Concerts in Italy, England, Belgium, Holland
              Begins *Ronsard à son âme* and orchestration of the
                  Hebrew *Chant populaire* (1910): both completed
                  Jan. 1924

1924 Apr.   First performance of *Tzigane*
     May   Concerts in Spain
     July   Orchestrates *Tzigane*
              Resumes work on *L'Enfant et les sortilèges*

1925 21 Mar. Première of *L'Enfant et les sortilèges* at Monte Carlo
              Begins *Chansons madécasses*

1926 Jan.–Feb. Concerts in Belgium, Scandinavia, Germany, England,
                  Scotland
     1 Feb.   Paris première of *L'Enfant et les sortilèges* at Opéra-
                  Comique
     Apr.   Completes *Chansons madécasses* (first performed June)
     Nov.   Concerts in Switzerland

FIGURES AND EVENTS IN THE ARTS

1923 First performances: *The Perfect Fool* (Holst), *Padmâvatî*
      (Roussel), *Les Noces* (Stravinsky)

1924 Nono born
      Busoni (58), Joseph Conrad (67), Fauré (79), Anatole France
          (80), Kafka (41), Puccini (66), Stanford (72) die
      First performances: *The Cunning Little Vixen* (Janáček), *Erwartung*
          and *Die glückliche Hand* (Schoenberg), *Intermezzo* (R. Strauss),
          Pacific 231 (Honegger)
      Breton publishes first *Surrealist Manifesto*

1925 Berio, Boulez born
      Satie (59) dies
      First performance of *Wozzeck* (Berg)
      Eisenstein's film *Battleship Potemkin*

1926 Feldman, Henze born
      Firbank (40), Monet (86), Rilke (51) die
      First performances: *The Makropoulos Case* (Janáček), *Háry János*
          (Kodály), *Turandot* (Puccini)

CONTEMPORARY EVENTS

1923 First Labour government in Britain
      Hitler attempts first *coup d'état* in Bavaria

1924 Birds Eye starts commercial production of frozen food

1925 Electric recording introduced

1926 General Strike in Britain

RAVEL'S LIFE AND WORKS

1927 May   First performance of Sonata for violin and piano
               Rêves. Fanfare for *L'Eventail de Jeanne*
               Sails for tour in USA and Canada

1928 4 Jan.   Arrives New York; 27 April returns to Le Havre
     July–Oct. *Boléro*, first performed at the Opéra in Nov.
     Oct.   Awarded Hon. D. Mus at Oxford University
     Nov.   Concerts in Spain

1929   Concerts in England, Switzerland, Austria
               Begins work on two piano concertos
               Orchestrates *Menuet antique*

FIGURES AND EVENTS IN THE ARTS

1927 Isadora Duncan (49) dies
     First performances: *Jonny spielt auf* (Křenek),
       Schwanda the bagpiper (Weinberger), *Oedipus Rex*
       (Stravinsky)
     First full-length talking film, *The Jazz Singer* with Al Jolson

1928 Barraqué, Stockhausen born
     Thomas Hardy (88), Janáček (74) die
     First performances: *Die ägyptische Helena* (R. Strauss),
       Die Dreigroschenoper (Weill)
     Dali's film *Le Chien andalou*
     Lady Chatterley's Lover (D. H. Lawrence) published in Paris

1929 John Osborne, Pousseur born
     Diaghilev (57), Hugo von Hofmannsthal (55) die
     First performances: *The Gambler* (Prokofiev),
       Sir John in Love (Vaughan Williams)

CONTEMPORARY EVENTS

1927 Lindbergh flies alone across the Atlantic
     Sacco and Vanzetti electrocuted in Massachusetts

1928 Kingsford-Smith flies across the Pacific
     Chiang Kai-Shek captures Peking and unites China

1929 Wall Street crash
     Allied Forces leave the Rhineland
     Trotsky exiled from Russia
     The word 'apartheid' first used in S. Africa

RAVEL'S LIFE AND WORKS

1930 Aug.   Inauguration of the Quai Maurice Ravel at Ciboure
              Completes Piano Concerto for the left hand

1931   Completes G major Concerto
      Nov.   Under doctor's orders to rest

1932 Jan.   First performances of left-hand Concerto in Vienna,
                  G major Concerto in Paris
              Sketches for *Morgiane*. Begins *Don Quichotte à
                  Dulcinée*
      Oct.   Taxi accident
      Dec.   Concert in Switzerland

1933   Completes *Don Quichotte à Dulcinée*
              First signs of fatal illness

1934   Enters Swiss clinic. Orchestrates *Don Quichotte*
      Dec.   First performance of *Don Quichotte*

FIGURES AND EVENTS IN THE ARTS

1930 D. H. Lawrence (45), Vladimir Mayakovsky (37) die
      First performances: *From the House of the Dead*
          (Janáček), *Christophe Colomb* (Milhaud), *Von Heute
          auf Morgen* (Schoenberg), *Aufstieg und Fall der Stadt
          Mahagonny* (Weill), *The Fairy's Kiss* (Stravinsky)

1931 Arnold Bennett (64), d'Indy (80) die

1933 Penderecki born
      Constantin Cavafy (70), Duparc (85), Stefan George (65) die
      First performance: *Arabella* (R. Strauss)

1934 Birtwistle, Maxwell Davies born
      Delius (72), Elgar (76), Holst (60) die
      First performances: *Lady Macbeth of Mtsensk*
          (Shostakovich), *Four Saints in Three Acts* (Virgil Thomson),
          Persephone (Stravinsky), *Paganini Rhapsody* (Rachmaninov)

CONTEMPORARY EVENTS

1930 Economic crisis hits Europe
      Allied Troops finally withdrawn from German soil

1931 Nylon invented

1932 First nuclear reaction activated
      Neutrons discovered

1933 Hitler appointed Chancellor of Germany by Hindenburg

1934 Austrian Chancellor Dollfuss murdered by Nazis
      In China the Long March begins

1935 Feb.   Leaves for tour of Spain and N. Africa with Léon
             Leyritz
     Aug.   Second visit to Spain

1936   Health deteriorates slowly

1937   Pain added to other symptoms
     19 Dec. Brain operation performed
     28 Dec. Ravel dies, aged 62

FIGURES AND EVENTS IN THE ARTS

1935 Berg (50), Dukas (69), T. E. Lawrence (47) die
      First performances: *Porgy and Bess* (Gershwin), *Die
         schweigsame Frau* (R. Strauss)
      Marx Brothers in *A Night at the Opera*

1936 Gilbert Amy born
      G. K. Chesterton (62), Glazunov (70), Kipling (71), Karl
         Kraus (62), Lorca (37), Pirandello (69), Respighi (56) die
      First television service opened in Britain

1937 Gershwin (38), Pierné (74), Roussel (68), Szymanowski (54) die
      First performances: *Lulu* (Berg), *Amelia Goes to the Ball*
         (Menotti), *Carmina Burana* (Orff), *Riders to the Sea*
         (Vaughan Williams)
      Picasso paints *Guernica*
      Paris Exhibition

CONTEMPORARY EVENTS

1935 Franco-Soviet pact
      Italy's Abyssinian war begins

1936 Abdication of Edward VIII
      Spanish Civil War
      Hitler re-militarizes the Rhineland
      Léon Blum heads Socialist government in France

1937 Fall of Blum government

I

Boyhood and student years

The Ravel family, *c* 1885: Edouard, Marie, Maurice and Joseph

Ravel at six years old

Maurice Ravel was born on 7 March 1875 in the village of Ciboure, just across the bay from Saint-Jean-de-Luz in the Basque region. His mother Marie, née Delouart, was of local stock but his father, Pierre Joseph Ravel, was Swiss – he met Marie in Aránjuez where he was working as a civil engineer on the construction of the railway. Three months after Maurice's birth the Ravel family moved to Paris, where a second son, Edouard, was born in 1878. Pierre Joseph was musical and had won a prize for piano playing at the Geneva Conservatory, so when Maurice too showed musical leanings no barriers were put in his way. He had his first piano lessons at the age of seven and in November 1889, at the age of fourteen and a half, he was accepted as a pupil at the Paris Conservatoire on the evidence of his playing of an excerpt from a Chopin concerto.

Ricardo VIÑES
(1876–1943)

Viñes was born in the Catalonian town of Lerida and in 1887 won a first prize for piano at the Barcelona Conservatory. He entered the Paris Conservatoire in 1889 at the same time as Ravel. He became Ravel's closest friend for some years and was to be one of the most notable interpreters of Ravel's piano music, giving the first performances of the *Menuet antique, Pavane pour une Infante défunte, Jeux d'eau, Miroirs* and *Gaspard de la nuit*. His diary gives a glimpse of their joint activities over a period of ten years.

November 1888
Thursday 23: I played a scale in thirds and octaves. In the evening we went for the first time to the home of the boy with long hair who is called Mauricio, 73 rue Pigalle on the 5th floor.

August 1892

Wednesday 10: to Ravel's after lunch. Not a moment's boredom. We played the piano a bit, talked, drew. Maurice showed me a very gloomy drawing he has done for a descent into Edgar Allan Poe's *Maelstrom*. When I was there today he did another one, also very black, for Poe's *Manuscript Found in a Bottle*.

Monday 15: to Ravel's in the afternoon. We didn't go out all day but enjoyed ourselves, almost all the time at the piano, trying out new chords and playing over our ideas. They made me stay to dinner. Edouard went to an exhibition of bicycles on the Champ de Mars[1]. After dinner we went out on to the balcony and looked at various constellations.

September 1894

Monday 17: I went to collect Ravel to go to poor Chabrier's funeral. When we reached his house, Ravel wanted to go back home and change his suit and hat because he didn't feel he was properly dressed.

October 1894

Wednesday 10: to Ravel's to take back the Baudelaire he lent me. There I saw the six poems from *Les Fleurs du mal* which have been condemned and banned: needless to say, they're the finest. One of Ravel's friends has lent him a copy, and when he has made his own he'll lend it to me so that I can do the same. Apart from that we sight-read a Mendelssohn organ sonata.

September 1896

Monday 14: I went to collect Ravel and we went off by boat to the exhibition at the Théâtre de la Musique so that he could see the piano with two keyboards, one of which is made going in the opposite direction to the other. He was overwhelmed by the sounds it produced.

---

[1] A large open space in front of the Eiffel Tower.

Ricardo Viñes and Ravel, *c* 1901

Friday 25: Ravel stayed till eleven in the evening. We read Sabatier's *Les Casques fleuris*, also Bertrand's *Gaspard de la nuit* which I let him take away.

November 1896

Sunday 1: Ravel and I went to the Concerts Lamoureux where we heard a singer very much of the Spanish type, Alba Chrétien, in an aria from *Oberon* and in 'Isolde's Liebestod'. No need to add that before that we heard the *Tristan* Prelude. By a strange coincidence, at the very moment when, feeling deeply moved, I was thinking to myself there was nothing in the whole of creation as sublime and divine as this superb Prelude, at that moment Ravel touched me on the hand and said: 'That's how it always is, every time I hear it . . .' and in fact he who looks so cold and cynical, Ravel the super-eccentric decadent, was trembling convulsively and crying like a child, really deeply too because every now and then I heard him sobbing.

Until now, in spite of the high opinion I had of Ravel's intellectual powers, I thought, because he is so secretive about the least details of his existence, that there was perhaps a touch of *parti pris* and fashion-following in his opinions and literary tastes. But since this afternoon I see that this fellow was born with inclinations, tastes and opinions and that when he expresses them he does so not to put on airs and be up to date but because he really feels that way; and I take this opportunity of declaring that Ravel is one of the most unlucky and misunderstood people of all because, in the eyes of the crowd, he passes for a failure, whereas in reality he is someone of superior intellect and artistic gifts, at odds with his surroundings and worthy of the greatest success in the future. He is, what's more, very complex: there is in him a mixture of medieval Catholicism and a satanic impiety, but he also has a love of art and beauty which guides him and makes him respond sincerely, as he showed today, weeping at the *Tristan* Prelude.

January 1897

Saturday 9: I went to Ravel's in the afternoon to lend him a *Rêverie* by Debussy. He introduced me to Chabrier's *La Sulamite* which is a pure marvel, late Chabrier of the best, most complete, complex and refined sort.

April 1897

Wednesday 28: to Ravel's, with whom I again played Rimsky-Korsakov's *Antar* arranged for piano duet, superbly Oriental music. He lent me *Les Diaboliques* by Barbey d'Aurevilly.

May 1897

Saturday 8: to Ravel's, who lent me *Du dandysme* and *De Brummel* by Barbey d'Aurevilly.

September 1897

Friday 17: Ravel came, bringing some Borodin which we read in a piano duet arrangement and also the sublime *Eolides* by César Franck.

Friday 24: to Ravel's where we sight-read duet arrangements of Rimsky-Korsakov symphonies and Debussy's *Proses lyriques* which are absolutely wonderful.

Monday 27: to Ravel's, who lends me Maeterlinck's *Nuits chaudes*, eight of which I have learnt by heart.

November 1897

Friday 19: What bizarre handwriting Ravel has! But very artistic. It denotes a creator, an intuitive type rather than a deductive one: the writing of a poet but not of someone with psychological insight. It shows a gift for satire and caustic irony.

December 1897

Sunday 19: at Ravel's we played a duet version of Balakirev's *Tamar*, a beautiful piece. I asked him to give me back *Gaspard de la nuit* and he said he would bring it around to my flat tomorrow because it was at the bottom of a trunk.

The composer's handwriting: a letter addressed to Mme Kriegel,
20 January 1926

April 1898

Saturday 2: Ravel came. I showed him my song *Parfum exotique* which he liked; not a negligible achievement for me, because he always finds faults and delivers his criticisms head on to the author. He simply remarked that the prosody was faulty, which I knew, but since I wrote it in the autumn of 1895 I haven't had time to correct it.

Ricardo Viñes
Diary entries in *Revue internationale de musique française*, 1/2, June 1980, pp. 183–95

Ravel remained at the Conservatoire until 1900, spending the last three of those years in Fauré's composition class. His earliest surviving works date from around 1893 and by the end of the decade he had produced a suite, *Sites auriculaires* for two pianos, a Violin Sonata, the overture *Shéhérazade* and the *Pavane pour une Infante défunte*.

Gustave MOUCHET

Nothing is known about Mouchet except that he was a fellow pupil of Ravel's at the Paris Conservatoire.

Shortly after the first performance of Massenet's *Werther* (in 1893), Ravel brought the score to Pessard's [1] class and before the professor's arrival started parodying the aria 'Pourquoi me réveiller, O souffle du printemps?'

Pour-quoi me ré - veil - ler,   O souffle du   prin - temps? __

---

[1] Emile Pessard (1843–1917) was Ravel's harmony teacher at the Conservatoire from 1891 to 1895.

playing it in the major mode and so bringing out its
resemblance to 'Ta-ra-ra-boom-de-ay' which we all started
singing in chorus.

Gustave Mouchet
as reported in *Le Guide musical*, Jan./Feb. 1938, p. 58

Alfred CORTOT
(1877–1962)

Alfred Cortot was a fellow pupil of Ravel's at the Conservatoire. He
went on to become one of the most famous pianists of his time.

. . . a deliberately sarcastic, argumentative and aloof
young man, who used to read Mallarmé and visit Erik
Satie.

Alfred Cortot
quoted in Roland-Manuel, *Maurice Ravel*, tr. Cynthia Jolly
(London, 1947), p. 25 (French edition *A la gloire de Ravel*
published Paris, 1938)

Louis AUBERT
(1877–1968)

Louis Aubert sang the treble solo in the first performance of Fauré's
Requiem in 1888. In 1911 he gave the first performance of Ravel's
Valses nobles et sentimentales for piano.

No one was freer than he was from obvious vanity.
Certainly he set great store, rather naïvely, by extreme
elegance in his clothes. But I wonder whether this was
not so much out of a desire to be noticed as to lose
himself in the anonymity of a certain bourgeois correct-

ness, and thus avoid the appearance of being an 'artist' which was then all the rage.

In the days when we were both in Fauré's composition class we lived close to each other and that was a further bond between us. Often, right at the end of the evening, our family gathering would be startled by a ring at the door, and someone would say: 'Ah! It's Ravel.' He might, for instance, have come to discuss some detail in writing for the harp, an instrument one of my sisters played. There was no instrument that he had not studied as thoroughly as was possible, and he pursued this knowledge with the single-mindedness of a man totally possessed by an exclusive passion.

Louis Aubert
ReM, Dec. 1938, pp. 206–7

Jane BATHORI
(1877–1970)

Jane Bathori was a well-known singer who specialized in the contemporary French repertoire. She gave first performances of several of Ravel's songs, including his *Histoires naturelles* in 1907.

I met Maurice Ravel in 1898. He was then a pupil in Fauré's class and, before speaking to me of what he was writing himself, he talked about Claude Debussy, for whom he professed a great admiration. At the time he wore a little pointed beard which exaggerated his pseudo-Spanish type. He was rather elaborate in the way in which he dressed. He liked to be the first to wear certain clothes – for example the double-breasted waistcoat; and at one time he started the mode for white socks and rather open patent shoes; but all this was done with great simplicity, and without consciously seeking to attract attention.

Ravel during his student days, *c* 1903

Going to London to sing and to play, we were at least six, and we were having a little meal in the train because restaurant cars did not exist then, each bringing his own share. Ravel arrived at the last minute with a grapefruit, which was a rarity then, and he had thought that he would give us a new pleasure which we should appreciate – a pleasure which we had to postpone until our arrival, having no receptacles or spoons. This way of going on was quite natural to Ravel. He had no desire to make himself conspicuous or to appear original. His musical ideas were the same and came from his brain in a manner that was absolutely personal to him.

Jane Bathori
'Les musiciens que j'ai connus', I, *Recorded Sound*, 5 (Autumn 1961), p. 150 (tr. Felix Aprahamian)

Tristan KLINGSOR
(1874–1966)

Tristan Klingsor (real name: Léon Leclère) was a French poet, painter and composer. Ravel set three poems from his collection *Shéhérazade* in 1903.

We were twenty-five years old. Ravel was still in Fauré's class at the Conservatoire. He was thin and hardy, given to mocking but secretly set in his purposes. That is how I always knew him. He seemed mysterious because he was too reticent to show the passion there was in him deep down. This ambitious dreamer liked to give an initial impression of being occupied with the surface of things and took delight in setting himself up as a dandy. With the most serious air you can imagine he would encourage us to admire his ties and socks and would enter on solemn disputations about their colour. I used to smile. I knew even then that he was not unhappy to cause astonishment. But our budding Beau Brummel had other means too . . . For example, when he called some early piano

pieces *Sites auriculaires*: it was under this title that
Ravel's name first appeared on a concert poster, for the
Société nationale de musique. Was the title deeply mean-
ingful, or a joke? We must remember this was the time of
Mallarmé and Jules Laforgue when Symbolists, decadents
and practical jokers shared between them the applause of
the few hundred people who made up the Paris that
mattered. They were all, including Ravel, happy to take
part in astonishing the bourgeoisie.

In our own gathering of artists it was the painter Paul
Sordes who did the talking; Ravel was the dreamer. If
some new work had to be sight-read, it was Sordes who
sat down at the piano; Ravel listened without moving.
He was comparing, inwardly analysing and, while
appearing to be idle, working and immersing himself
ever more deeply in the magical, mathematical world of
music. He used to keep his thoughts to himself. When
occasionally he used to express them, seriousness was
soon leavened with mockery. His voice sounded clear and
bantering, his eyes sparkled and his curved mouth
executed a mischievous smile. But never sarcastic. His
mockery was reserved for bumpkins who composed
rubbish instead of that unique blend of sensitivity and
spirituality which, for him, was what music consisted of.

Tristan Klingsor
Maurice Ravel par quelques-uns de ses familiers (Paris, 1939),
pp. 125–6, 128, 129

Jacques-Emile BLANCHE
(1861–1942)

Jacques-Emile Blanche was a fashionable portrait painter. His father ran the most expensive mental institution in Paris.

That Friday in Mme de Saint-Marceaux's[1] salon Fauré and Messager had just provoked roars of laughter with their quadrille for piano duet on themes from Wagner's *Ring*. The cream of musical society was there. Vincent d'Indy's frock coat struck the only sombre note in a brightly coloured gathering, with young ladies willing to oblige with a chorus: Chabrier, perhaps, or Brahms' *Liebeslieder* Waltzes.

Willy and Colette[2] were there, as usual. A strange little fellow – a newcomer – was nervously turning the pages of some score, Russian probably, which a pianist was sight-reading. Standing there, a compact figure in his short jacket, he looked like an aficionado of the bull-ring or a horsetrainer's lad. Who was he? 'Maurice Ravel', said Debussy, without expatiating on his future rival.

Soon I got to know this amazing musician better. He was not always prepared to do his bit in playing the innumerable works, both classical and modern, that enthusiastic guests found in their hostess's enormous library. Myself, having been surrounded by music since childhood, I felt a rather tiresome need to be always discovering things, instead of enjoying and improving my knowledge of what I knew, like most music-lovers.

I was looking for a piano duet partner to replace a cousin with whom I had spent hours reading through scores. Mme de Saint-Marceaux recommended Ravel who, like most of his comrades, was eking out a living giving music lessons and doing other things beside composing. There was also talk of Ravel giving me harmony lessons but, thank Heaven, no such calamity ensued! We agreed, though, that he would come twice a week to my

---

[1] She was one of the leading musical hostesses of Paris.
[2] See pp. 56–8.

studio to play duets. These meetings were planned, postponed and finally abandoned, for the curious reason that Ravel asked me to exclude Beethoven, Wagner, Schumann and any other 'romantics' from our repertoire and indicated we should stick to the numerous works of Mozart. I was not very happy with the idea and roused in him a mixture of disdain and pity. Although I could smile at his obsessive rejections and enthusiasms, he could do no such thing at my indifference towards Couperin and Rameau.

I emphasize this because I think it is important. No one seems to have had the slightest influence in any respect or in any field on Ravel's opinions. Once he had made up his mind he was immovable – sometimes childishly pig-headed in his determination to be contrary; so much so that you might have taken him for a hoaxer or even had doubts about his intelligence.

Jacques-Emile Blanche
ReM, Dec. 1938, pp. 186–7

II

A child at heart

The ability to retain the images and directness of childhood has often lain at the heart of great artists' work. Ravel went one further in seeming to prefer the company of children to that of adults; Mme Ibert has recalled noticing his absence suddenly at a *soirée* and finding him on the floor of the nursery in earnest conversation with his hostess's children.

Mimi GODEBSKA
(1899–1949)

Mimi Godebska was the daughter of Ravel's friends Cipa and Ida Godebski, to whom he dedicated his *Sonatine*. Cipa's half-sister Misia was to become one of Diaghilev's closest confidantes. Ravel regularly used to stay at the Godebskis' country house, La Grangette, at Valvins, as well as visiting them in their Paris flat on the rue d'Athènes.

There are few of my childhood memories in which Ravel does not find a place. Of all my parents' friends I had a predilection for Ravel because he used to tell me stories that I loved. I used to climb on his knee and indefatigably he would begin, 'Once upon a time . . .' And it would be *Laideronnette* or 'Beauty and the Beast' or, especially, the adventures of a poor mouse that he made up for me. I used to laugh uproariously at these and then feel guilty because they were really very sad.

There was a childish side to Ravel and a warmth of feeling which remained almost invisible beneath his *pudeur*. It was in curious contrast to his face which was energetic, even unyielding, and to his music in which logic and wit did not always succeed in disguising the promptings of his heart. He loved tiny things. He and my

Ricardo Viñes playing at the Godebskis'. Cipa Godebski is the bearded man
sitting behind Viñes. Ravel is leaning on the piano at far right. The standing
figures, from left to right, are Florent Schmitt, Déodat de Séverac, M. D.
Calvocoressi and Albert Roussel. Painting by Georges d' Espagnat

brother used to enjoy silly practical jokes and often
discussed men's fashions. He was extremely meticulous
in the choice of his suits and ties. I often found myself
looking at his hands: artisan's hands, intelligent and
precise, with long fingers squared off at the ends, dry and
unsupple, which possibly explained his lack of virtuosity
at the piano, something he was the first to laugh at.

When my parents moved into their flat on the rue
d'Athènes, Ravel took a room in a very modest hotel
opposite where he used to stay when he came to Paris
from Montfort. He used to have all his meals free and
generally arrived late – for dinner, often long after we
had finished and the servants had gone to bed. Then he
used to apologize to my mother, whom he adored: 'I'm
sorry, Ida, give me a little of whatever's going, I'm not at
all hungry today.' Mama would give me a meaning smile
and I would go and do the necessary. On those evenings
we knew that was the end of the next day's cold meat.

Ravel and my father were close friends: they admired and understood each other wholeheartedly. Even so they often argued violently and where music was concerned their great bone of contention was Mozart. To try and convince my father, Ravel would usually go to the piano and play a phrase which he thought was 'pure genius'. Papa, noisy and larger than life, would reply, 'Yes, yes, but he bores me with all that repetition, those fiddle-de-dees and fol-de-rols that go on and on.'

Between 1906 and 1908 we used to have long holidays at my parents' house in the country, La Grangette at Valvins. It was there that Ravel finished, or at least brought us, *Ma Mère l'Oye*. But neither my brother nor I was of an age to appreciate such a dedication and we regarded it rather as something entailing hard work. Ravel wanted us to give the first public performance but the idea filled me with a cold terror. My brother, being less timid and more gifted on the piano, coped quite well. But despite lessons from Ravel I used to freeze to such an extent that the idea had to be abandoned.

At Christmas Ravel used to bring us loads of little toys. He loved surprises and magic and got as much pleasure as we did out of the toys and mechanical objects on sale at the New Year on the stalls of the boulevards. He liked the Rococo and the Baroque and was enchanted by a certain kind of bad taste. He often used to bring my mother miniature Japanese gardens with dwarf oak-trees in – they were so full of strength and violence that when you looked at them through opera-glasses they seemed gigantic. In any game of 'Suppose', if it came to 'Suppose he were a tree' I could describe Ravel without any hesitation at all!

It was he who made me read the *Fioretti*[1] of St Francis of Assisi.

---

[1] The *Fioretti* is an early fourteenth-century compilation of legends and anecdotes about the life of St Francis of Assisi (1182–1226) along with his sermons and sayings.

Although he was a confirmed atheist he adored this book , and I was so amazed by it that I used to imagine it being set to music – by Ravel.

Mimi Godebska Blacque-Belair
ReM, Dec. 1938, pp. 189–91

III

*Opinions,
tastes and traits*

Ravel as a young man

Emile VUILLERMOZ
(1878–1960)

Emile Vuillermoz was a prominent critic. He was one of the group known as 'Les Apaches' and in 1910 was a founder member of the *Société musicale indépendante.*

Critics, photographers, writers and engravers have only ever given misleading and contradictory portraits of him. His bold nose, his thin lips, his hermetic mouth, his lively, cruel eyes, his face, with lines which are always exaggerated in reproduction, the shape of his head modelled by some sculptor with a strong thumb, the stern, unyielding lines of his thin, machine-like body, his skin tanned like that of a retired sailor – all these together form a disconcerting ensemble. One is usually aware with him of isolated details which don't fit in with each other. He is a child and he is an old man. He will laugh at a trifle but his drawn face can easily take on a severe, closed expression. He moves instantly from gentle lightheartedness to gloomy gravity. He often gives the impression of being in pain. His tormented features and furrowed brow bear witness to some indefinable struggle of conscience; some inexplicable core of sorrow resides there. One thinks of those dwarf trees from Japan which, in spite of their smallness, offer a tragic concentration, in their contorted branches and roughened bark, of all the fierce battles that the forest giants have to fight against the ferocity of the elements and the seasons. He looks sly and nervous, like a fox cub or a little mouse scenting danger everywhere; which is surprising in such a lucid, determined, precise artist with nothing to fear from life.

Emile Vuillermoz
Les Cahiers d'aujourd'hui, no. 10, 1922, quoted in Marcel Marnat, *Maurice Ravel* (Paris, 1986), pp. 522–3

Ravel was born on the Côte d'Argent at Ciboure, a pretty little village not far from Saint-Jean-de-Luz and in 1930 the inhabitants decided to set up a commemorative plaque on the house in which their illustrious son had been born. Ravel was there for the ceremony, which was particularly affecting in its simple cordiality. Wearing a little Basque beret and surrounded by a crowd of fisher-men and pelota players, all acclaiming him vigorously without ever, alas, having heard a note of his music, Ravel renewed contact with the spirit of his race. His short stature, his lean, wiry figure, his agile gestures and his flashing eyes, everything about him proclaimed his distant origins. I shall always see him, sitting in the front row on a makeshift stage, looking out over a large pelota court on which his compatriots, unconsciously renewing the touching gesture of the juggler of Notre-Dame, presented the composer with their most prized offering: a game of pelota, played with the utmost energy and enthusiasm.

Superficial observers who met this frail-looking man with his emaciated face and prematurely white hair, caring passionately about the knots in his ties and kissing the hands of aristocratic ladies, took him for a descendant of those worldly abbés who flitted through the musical salons of the eighteenth century. They did not realize that this fragile appearance disguised a robust good health and a silent but vibrant energy. Ravel knew what he wanted and followed his path with an inflexible logic.

Emile Vuillermoz
ReM, Dec. 1938, pp. 54, 55

Léon-Paul FARGUE
(1876–1947)

Léon-Paul Fargue was a writer, one of the 'Apaches' and the dedicatee of 'Noctuelles' from Ravel's *Miroirs*. He was probably the closest friend Ravel ever had.

From his mother's side he inherited a physique that was specifically Basque; the small stature, the thinness, the vivacity of his presence, the bony regularity of his face

Léon-Paul Fargue

and the deep sockets, separated by the long aquiline nose, in which shone two eyes alive with understanding.

Thousands of his admirers saw him for the last time conducting a concert in the provinces at which Marguerite Long was playing the Concerto for the left hand. With his small body dressed in a grey woollen suit to match the thick silver of his hair, he looked like a distinguished jockey who had replaced his whip with a baton. His long, narrow, bony hands made rather stiff gestures; they were not pianist's hands and went some way towards explaining why his piano playing tended to be dry and why he loathed making an 'exhibition' of himself. When he went to America he had a rapturous reception but contented himself with public performances only of the *Sonatine* and the Violin Sonata, and with accompanying his songs.

Even when he was wasted by illness, Ravel never appeared unkempt even among his closest friends. All his life he kept the perfect, discriminating taste which led him to match his braces to his blue or pink silk shirts, much to the astonishment of performers whom he would rehearse in his shirtsleeves (for a long time he went on wearing a grey tie with his dinner jacket and a grey waistcoat with his evening dress). In Chicago a major concert was delayed for nearly an hour because Ravel refused to appear on the podium without his evening shoes, which were still by mistake in the left-luggage office.

He attached little importance to honours or fame but was sensitive to true, spontaneous demonstrations of enthusiasm. He used to love telling of the time he went to one of the best leather shops in Vienna to buy a wallet. When he came to pay he gave his name and the address of his hotel. The salesgirl asked him, in excellent French, if he was indeed Ravel the composer of *Jeux d'eau*, which she loved playing. When he said he was, she replied, 'Then, *maître*, allow me to offer you this wallet with my thanks and in token of my profound admiration.'

Ravel used to say: 'Vienna is the only city where a salesgirl would play *Jeux d'eau* and make you such a gracious gesture.'

Léon-Paul Fargue
Maurice Ravel (Paris, 1949), pp. 28–32

André SUARÈS
(1868–1948)

André Suarès was a French writer whose early enthusiasm for Beethoven and Wagner was tempered by a gradual appreciation of Debussy, of whom he wrote a biography in 1922.

I remember Ravel on a small stage, sitting at the piano. He was accompanying some songs for female voice, flute and harp. A tiny man[1], delicate, with a matt complexion and hair almost entirely and prematurely white; nervous and hiding his nerves with difficulty; detached and unostentatiously elegant; more sensitive than he liked to appear; his face clean-shaven, his hands nimble and decisive using what seemed to be idiosyncratic fingering – I was amazed by this face which looked so oddly French and Spanish at the same time. His head was a cube, the front of it squared off and, were it not for the eyes, you would have said it belonged to a scholar or a poet rather than a musician. But his eyes, large, sad and serious, meditating under their strongly arched brows, fixed their attention on an object and considered it at length. I will go so far as to say that Ravel's head suggests to me that of a younger brother of Baudelaire. What in Baudelaire is profundity and suffering brought to the intensity of a passion, with Ravel is obsession, long application and unease veiled by melancholy.

There was never anything Italian in Ravel's music; he despised facility and the making of effects. All the Mediterranean in him came from Spain, governed by a French wit and a Parisian intellect. No one, except possibly Debussy, was further from being a barbarian.

André Suarès
ReM, Dec. 1938, pp. 49, 50

---

[1] He was about 5 ft. 4 in.

Marguerite LONG
(1878–1966)

Marguerite Long was born in Nîmes and studied at the Paris
Conservatoire with the younger Marmontel. She herself was
appointed Professor of Piano there in 1920. She made many
recordings of French music, including one of Ravel's G major
Concerto with the composer conducting.

When we turn from a genius to consider the man we
often do so with apprehension. The transcendent
qualities of the former make such demands on the latter.
But with Ravel such contemplation reveals marvellous
treasures among which seem to be combined Schubert's
friendliness, Mendelssohn's courtesy, Liszt's generosity,
and Albéniz's delicacy. I think I will not have difficulty
in avoiding the reproach that mine is a partial opinion of
the kind to which one is prone in studying someone
extraordinary. There is no risk when diverse impressions
are gleaned. Approbation is general and comes from the
greatest and from the most modest – those who still say of
him at Montfort, or in the Basque country: 'What a nice
man M. Ravel was!'

His features and his manner have often been described
but it must be said that neither pencil, brush, nor chisel
has ever succeeded fully in delineating them. He could
have been called – someone once said – 'the despair of
painters'.

He was a typical Basque; small, thin, the bone structure
of his face strongly marked, and ascetic. His hair was
wavy, and having turned early to silver gave an expression
of gentleness to his energetic features. He had a youthful
figure and his walk was supple and elastic. An indefatigable walker, he was like his great friend, Fargue, much
given to walking about Paris. His eyes were brown and
deep set. Their expression, open and enquiring, was
welcoming, yet often alert to signal imminent danger.
His mouth was thin, hinting at reserve, and perhaps
uneasiness. When he smiled, it sometimes seemed to

Marguerite Long

suggest mocking but at times it was dark with shadow. What were his fears? What secret grief did he nourish?

He was something of a dandy, anxious to follow fashion or even to set it. He dressed very carefully and he had a penchant for nice ties, the choice of which was often the subject of endless discussion. This trait, very marked early on, and the constant, meticulous elegance which followed, helped Ravel to create an appearance and to carry the mask he ever used to thwart all invasion of his privacy. His small stature troubled him much; not very noticeable when he was sitting down, it became so when he stood up. Should there be even a veiled and involuntary allusion to his stature (such as the 'Petit Ravel, it is your birthday today,' that someone uttered at Montfort on the day when Leyritz delivered his bust) he immediately shut himself up in a sad, stolid silence. To some admirer who enquired about his physique he replied: 'He is very big and has the appearance of a cavalry officer', but in an aside he murmured: 'Some composers were small: think of Beethoven and Mozart.'

Ravel's integrity and loyalty were beyond reproach. He showed anger only when aroused by the discovery of dishonesty or some 'dirty trick'. He never wanted to hurt those who bore him ill-will, indeed he was incapable of hurting. He was always free from untruth and malice. Although he was very generous and helpful so long as no one knew of his generosity, Ravel was neglectful of his own financial interests in spite of the attempts that Stravinsky once made to make him aware of them.

It might be thought that he refused the Legion of Honour and election to the Institut de France out of rancour for the officials who had so disgracefully refused him the Prix de Rome, but he was really without any ambition other than to make good music, and he never put himself under obligation for self-interest.

So far as manners were concerned he was a complete thoroughbred, but he detested vulgarity and over-familiarity. He had the same consideration for people of little importance as for the great, to whom he showed no special regard, for he offered to all human beings their share of dignity.

Taking all this into account what place had Ravel for love? It seemed that there was none. His morbid reserve, the inferiority complex on account of his smallness, and his extended childhood were hardly the best preparation. One day I said to him: 'Maurice, you ought to marry. Nobody understands and loves children as you do. Get rid of your hermit life and have a real home.' Ravel replied: 'Love never rises above the licentious.' This 'licentiousness' he was willing, within moderation, to allow to some street-walking Venus; what remained beyond that would have turned his life upside-down and he did not find the idea an encouraging one.

Marguerite Long
At the Piano with Ravel (London, 1973), tr. Olive Senior-Ellis, pp. 117–19, 121. (French edition *Au piano avec Ravel* published in Paris, 1971)

Manuel ROSENTHAL
(born 1904)

Manuel Rosenthal studied composition with Ravel after the First
World War and was a close friend until Ravel's death. He has
conducted the French National Radio Orchestra regularly and his
Ravel recordings are models of style and understanding. He has
orchestrated three of the *Cinq mélodies populaires grecques* (nos. 2,
3 and 4).

Any number of legends have gathered round him, nonsense like the make-up Alma Mahler claims to have seen
on his face . . .[1] Perhaps one morning, as a tease to
provoke her, he did put a touch of rouge on his cheeks,

Manuel Rosenthal, 1936

[1] See p. 147.

Ida Rubinstein

we don't know. Anything is possible. But his emotional
life was in fact utterly simple and unhappy. He was very
conscious both of his short stature and of his position as
an artist. One day we were both walking along the
Boulevard d'Auteuil and there was a silence for a quarter
of an hour. I always respected his silences, naturally,
being young, and never took it upon myself to start a
conversation or ask him a question. And after this long
silence he suddenly said: 'You see, an artist has to be very
careful when he wants to marry someone, because an
artist never realizes his capacity for making his companion miserable. He's obsessed by his creative work and
by the problems it poses. He lives a bit like a daydreamer
and it's no joke for the woman he lives with. One always
has to think of that when one wants to get married.'

I also discovered, from things he let slip and from what
his great friend the violinist Hélène Jourdan-Morhange
confided to me, that one day he asked her to marry him.
As she told me, she was quite frank: 'No, Maurice, I'm
extremely fond of you, as you know, but only as a friend,
and I couldn't possibly consider marrying you.' And that
was that.

He liked women very much and was always exquisitely
polite and kind to them. Sometimes his kindness to them
was put to the test, as in the case of his brother Edouard's
wife, who was rather nondescript, a rather ugly, vulgar
woman. But he used to treat her like a queen. He never
went on a journey without bringing her back some
present, an unusual fan, something very special. His
greatest female friend, a wonderful woman, was Ida
Rubinstein. He liked her discretion. She was very rich
but absolutely never showed it. She was a very private
woman and, with Ravel, she behaved like a little girl,
which he adored. It was really quite funny to see them
together, he so tiny and she so tall. She was a very
beautiful woman, tall, very slim, a kind of legendary
figure (*Le Martyre de Saint Sébastien* . . .)[1]. And with

---

[1] Ida Rubinstein had played the role of the saint in d'Annunzio's drama, produced in
Paris in 1911 with music by Debussy.

Ravel she was like a little girl. He only had to mention something, or point to something, for her, in the discreetest possible way, to issue a command and what Ravel wanted was promptly bought, regardless of cost, naturally . . . She was so happy to please him and to be able, thanks to her wealth, to procure for Ravel things he couldn't afford, not being at all well off.

At other times he and I used to meet, not at Levallois-Perret, where he had a studio in the house occupied by his brother, but in a large *brasserie* by the Porte Champerret. The first time, when I expressed surprise at being asked to meet in a large *brasserie*, he said, 'That's where I'll be from eleven o'clock and, you'll see, it's very nice, there are ladies there'. What he called 'ladies' were, in fact, prostitutes and indeed when I arrived there with Ravel to have an aperitif, before we both went off to Montfort l'Amaury, I saw several of these 'ladies' making signs at him; they knew him very well and he gave them a very friendly wave, saying 'Bonjour, bonjour'. I think it was a sort of outlet. Being conscious of his smallness and of his position as a creative artist, he turned to prostitutes. It was very understandable and, for me anyway, completely refutes the suggestion people have made – without any sort of proof, and indeed I have proof to the contrary, as you see – that he was homosexual. Not that it would have mattered in the least: he could have been homosexual without prejudice to his musical genius, but he wasn't.

He was a subscriber to Léon Blum's[1] paper, *Le Populaire*. His views were, as we would say today, leftish, that's to say he was totally opposed to all social inequality. In Montfort l'Amaury he was adored by the lower classes because he was immediately on their level. He was never paternalistic, he spoke their language because he considered himself to be a worker, an artisan. He never thought of himself as an artist, an intellectual: those words used to make him furious. He used his

---

[1] Prominent Socialist politician who was Prime Minister in 1936–7.

money in a very practical, discreet way, but that was part of his ability not to make efforts to sympathize with people, but to find himself quite naturally on their level. And I may say that when the first refugees from Hitler's Germany arrived in Paris, simply because he had composed the *Chants hébraïques* – even though he had no Jewish blood in him – Jews expelled from Germany came and rang his doorbell in Montfort l'Amaury to ask for help. And I discovered, not from him, of course, but from his housekeeper, Mme Revelot, that considering his own slender resources he used to give them extremely substantial cheques.

Manuel Rosenthal
interview with Rémy Stricker, 'France Culture', 1985, quoted in Marcel Marnat, *Maurice Ravel* (Paris, 1986), pp. 462–5, 674

Ricardo VIÑES

Debussy and Ravel were both sybarites and devoted gourmets. Debussy was perhaps the less voracious of the two, whereas Ravel distinguished himself by consuming alarming doses of pickles, pepper, mustard and other stimulating condiments which he was able to stomach, and by his marked preference for exotic and Oriental dishes.

As for the view, the assertion indeed, that Ravel was politically very far to the left, I must admit that the real essence of the man has always seemed to me to resist definition, and that his complex, even contradictory character makes nonsense of attempts to classify it. Even so, I think one can sum it up impartially by saying that the tastes and natural propensities of this extraordinary artist had almost nothing in common with what he thought he was or what he *wanted* to be. All through his youth his favourite authors were, principally, Joseph

de Maistre, Baudelaire, Huysmans, Edgar Allan Poe,
Barbey d'Aurevilly and Villiers de l'Isle Adam. What
could be plainer or more revelatory?

Ricardo Viñes
ReM, Dec. 1938, pp. 170, 171

Piero COPPOLA
(1888–1971)

Piero Coppola was born and studied in Milan. In 1922 he came to
Paris to be artistic director of Le Gramophone, the French branch of
HMV. He was also very active as a conductor, especially with the
Pasdeloup Orchestra.

Although half-Basque and half-Swiss by birth, he was
and remained utterly French; and like any good French-
man he was sad to see the decline of France that has
brought it to its present pass. After warning me that
'Frenchmen don't like music', he went on to say, 'In
France they don't like hard work, so don't put yourself to
any trouble.' And of the old French traditions he said,
'Believe me, they're dead. All people dream about are
Citroëns, football matches and patriotic plays!'

Piero Coppola
Dix-sept ans de musique à Paris, 1922–1939 (Paris, 2nd edn,
1982), pp. 216–17

IV

Daphnis et Chloé
and
Boléro

Mikhail Fokine, drawing by V. Serov

The years between 1905 and 1914 saw the composition of some of Ravel's greatest and best-known works: *Miroirs* (1905), *Rapsodie espagnole* (1907–8), *Gaspard de la nuit* (1908), *Ma Mère l'Oye* (1908–10), *Valses nobles et sentimentales* (1911) and the Piano Trio (1914). But none of these gave Ravel such trouble as the ballet *Daphnis et Chloé*, commissioned by Diaghilev in 1909 for the Ballets Russes, who gave the work its première on 8 June 1912.

Mikhail FOKINE
(1880–1942)

Mikhail Fokine was trained at the Imperial Theatre School in St Petersburg and staged his first ballet in 1905. His most famous achievements were undoubtedly as the choreographer of *Carnaval, The Firebird, Le Spectre de la rose, Petrushka* and *Daphnis et Chloé*. He and his family left Russia in 1918 and finally settled in New York.

When, in the summer of 1910 in Paris, Serge Diaghilev asked me whether I had any libretto for a ballet which could be staged the following season, I told him the story of *Daphnis et Chloé*. He, and especially Léon Bakst, were pleased with the libretto. Diaghilev commissioned Maurice Ravel to write the music for the ballet and introduced me to the composer.

The rather youthful Ravel (he was thirty-five) was not yet the famous master, the leader of the modern French composers, which he was destined to become later. He invited me to his house to get acquainted with his music. On an upright piano which was standing, as I recall it, in the dining room of his modest apartment, he played his Undine[1] for me. I was greatly stirred by the Undine

---

[1] 'Ondine', the first movement of Ravel's *Gaspard de la nuit*.

music and even thought that it should be produced as a
ballet. I was delighted that a musician of such talent was
going to write music for my *Daphnis* ballet, and I felt
that the music would be unusual, colourful and, most
important, what I sincerely wished – totally unlike any
other ballet music.

I brought Bakst along to our next meeting to act as my
interpreter, as my French at that time was not very
fluent. I related to Ravel the libretto of *Daphnis et Chloé*
and told him how I saw the action and visualized the
music. I expressed my belief in the necessity of uninter-
rupted movement and the unity of the performance as a
whole, and spoke of my wish to avoid separate numbers;
also of the desirability – even in part – of communicating
the character of the music of antiquity, and so forth.

At one time I had dreamed of hearing in *Daphnis*, for
the very first time in the modern theatre, the resurrected
music of ancient Greece. But in the course of my conversations with Ravel I realized that information on the
music of the ancient world is very scarce, and that no
resurrection is possible. By that time I had begun to
think that it was not even necessary.

I had become acquainted with the views of Nicholas
Rimsky-Korsakov on the impossibility of restoration of
ancient music – which he expressed on the occasion of
the composition of his opera *Servilia* – and limited
myself to the desire that there should be no obvious
contradictions and noticeable disagreements with the
character of the Graeco-Roman art. Of course it was
unnecessary for me to ask Ravel to refrain from the
traditional forms of the old ballet music, as I had had to
do in the case of my first music collaborator, A. V.
Kadletz. To begin with, Ravel was not involved with the
old tradition of ballet. And, in the second place, having
seen a series of my productions he was already very well
aware that polkas, pizzicatos, waltzes, and galops – so
indispensable in the old ballet – were completely out of
place in the new. That is why he had agreed to compose
the music for this one.

Total freedom in creation – freedom in choice of musical form, measure, and rhythms, and in the length of the individual parts – gave him a joyful opportunity to begin his composition of the music, a task which, under former conditions, most composers had shunned.

I tried to collaborate with Ravel to the minutest detail in conveying the various moments of action. It was essential for me to have him feel exactly as I did at each moment of this romance of a shepherd and a shepherdess on the Isle of Lesbos. It was equally important that we both should understand the meaning of each dance in the same way.

After holding several conferences and, as I recollect it, reaching an accord with me, Ravel began to compose. Only at one point did we have different views. I planned to make an elaborate dramatic sequence out of the attack of the pirates. I felt that the slaying of the shepherds, the abduction of the women, the plunder of the cattle, would all contribute to the unfolding of interesting action. Ravel, however, wanted to produce a lightning attack. I yielded, realizing that this was the way he felt at that moment, and that, probably due to my limitations in the French language, I was unable to inspire him to create musically that violent, gruesome picture which was so vivid in my imagination. I later came to reproach myself for not having insisted on this point. I had displayed an unusual timidity in an artistic matter, and have since become convinced that such an attitude is a liability. It is far better to be a stubborn, uncooperative character; it is even better to have a quarrel (of very short duration, of course) than to depart from one's convictions if one believes them to be the truth.

Ravel familiarized me with the music when it was completely ready. With the exception of the scene just mentioned, which was even shorter than I expected, I loved the score from the time I first heard it.

Mikhail Fokine
Memoirs of a Ballet Master (London, 1961), tr. V. Fokine, pp. 195–6, 199

René CHALUPT

René Chalupt edited a volume of Ravel's letters in 1956, with the help of the singer Marcelle Gerar. He was also a poet in a small way; Satie and Milhaud set some of his verses to music.

He claimed his music was extremely simple. 'Nothing is simpler,' he used to say, 'than the dawn music in *Daphnis et Chloé*. It's just a pedal-point held by three flutes and the theme develops, especially in its harmonic context, like *En revenant de la revue*.'

René Chalupt
Ravel au miroir de ses lettres (Paris, 1956), p. 267

Manuel ROSENTHAL

When I asked Ravel about the finale of *Daphnis*, he said, 'Yes, I was in a very bad mood over it, so much so that I put Rimsky's *Sheherazade* on the piano and tried, very humbly, to write something like it.'

Manuel Rosenthal
in conversation with the editor

Boléro was first given as a ballet by Ida Rubinstein's troupe at the Paris Opéra on 22 November 1928. The conductor was Walther Straram, the décor and costumes were by Alexandre Benois and the choreography by Nijinsky's sister Bronislava Nijinska.

Joaquín NIN
(1879–1949)

Joaquín Nin was born in Havana and studied at the Schola Cantorum in Paris, where he taught the piano from 1905 to 1908. He was active as composer, pianist and conductor.

On one occasion in the summer of 1928 I asked Ravel, out of idle curiosity, what he was planning to work on next. He told me that he was going to orchestrate some of the numbers from Albéniz's *Iberia* for Ida Rubinstein to dance to. The commission interested him and he was all set up to fulfil it. But . . . I pointed out to Ravel that unfortunately this project could not go forward as Albéniz's pieces had already been orchestrated by Arbós[1] for a ballet to be danced by La Argentina: it was *Triana*, given the following season with enormous success. Ravel made light of the problem, saying simply: 'I don't give a damn . . . Who is this Arbós?' As far as Arbós was concerned I guessed Ravel was just being a tease, as so often, and went on to explain as clearly as I could that the publishers Max Eschig would undoubtedly have taken all necessary steps to ensure their exclusive rights over the ballet and that no other work based on these pieces could therefore be performed. I realized that my explanations were beginning to make Ravel edgy. Silence reigned over the matter.

Two cigarettes later I suddenly had the idea of distracting him by asking what models of orchestration I ought to study to get as close as possible to the Spanish nuances. The reply was prompt and categorical. 'Look at my scores, and Rimsky's and some of Debussy's. But not d'Indy or Wagner . . . ! (I waited motionless) . . . and a few moments later he added quietly: 'Look at Meyerbeer too.' I was incredulous. Meyerbeer? 'Yes, Meyerbeer. It's Wagner, but good Wagner.' (I hope I shall be pardoned this aside, which has nothing to do with *Boléro*, but which I thought was worth quoting.)

---

[1] Enrique Arbós, the Spanish violinist, conductor and composer.

The next morning we came back to the question of *Iberia* and once again I begged Ravel not to embark on a project which, in the eyes of the law at least, was bound to be a waste of time. He was still sceptical but now in a more reasonable frame of mind, so he asked me to contact Eschig and find out whether he could go ahead with the orchestration or not. The next day I telephoned Eugène Cools who was then the managing director. His reply was definitive: the ballet, like the scenario and the music, was covered by a network of agreements, signatures and copyrights that could not be broken. No one except Enrique Arbós could touch Albéniz's *Iberia*. This time Ravel could not hide his displeasure: 'My whole summer's wrecked'; 'The law is an ass'; 'I have to work'; 'Orchestrating *Iberia* was going to be such fun'; 'Who is this Arbós?'; 'What am I going to tell Ida? She'll be furious!' and so on for the rest of the day. I have rarely seen Ravel more jumpy or put out. Two days later he announced that he was going back to Paris to see Ida Rubenstein and decide with her what to do next; adding, for the benefit of the world at large, that he loved being in Paris for 14 July.

Some weeks passed with no news from him (which was quite normal) and then one day I had a short letter saying that he was working at something rather unusual: 'No form in the true sense of the word, no development, hardly any modulation; a theme in the style of Padilla (the terribly vulgar composer of 'Valencia') together with rhythm and orchestration . . .' It was the *Boléro*.

The following year Ravel was kind enough to give me an inscribed copy of the score. '*Boléro* is to some extent your fault,' he said. 'If you hadn't warned me I'd have put myself heart and soul into orchestrating *Iberia*, and think how awful that would have been.' Then he added, almost as a confidence: 'Be careful how you use the oboe d'amore: it didn't work out as I hoped!'

Joaquín Nin
ReM, Dec. 1938, pp. 211–13

Hélène JOURDAN-MORHANGE
(1892–1961)

Hélène Jourdan-Morhange was a violinist. She gave first performances of Ravel's *Berceuse sur le nom de Fauré* and, with Maurice
Maréchal, of the Sonata for violin and cello, both in 1922. A few
years later rheumatism put an end to her career. She was one of
Ravel's closest friends in the last years of his life. She was married to
the artist Luc-Albert Moreau.

Ravel was extremely surprised at the mass success of
Boléro. 'They're going to turn it into another *Madelon*,'[1]
he said, rather crossly; and deep down he felt that the
obsessive, musico-sexual element in the piece was
probably behind its enormous popularity. But one old
lady was proof against the contagion. Ravel's brother
Edouard saw her, at the first performance, wedged
tightly in her seat shouting above the applause 'Rubbish!

Ravel, Hélène Jourdan-Morhange and Ricardo Viñes on the beach
at St-Jean-de-Luz, 1923

[1] The favourite song of the French soldiers during the latter part of the First World
War.

Rubbish!' Maurice, when informed by his brother, replied mysteriously: 'That old lady got the message!'

Hélène Jourdan-Morhange
Ravel et nous (Geneva, 1945), p.166

Jane BATHORI

He was always very simple and was a delightful friend. He never sought honours: on the contrary, sometimes he asked himself what people saw in his music, for instance one day he said to me, 'I've composed a Bolero for Ida Rubinstein – it's a little thing. Ansermet finds it very good, I really can't think why.'

Jane Bathori
'Les musiciens que j'ai connus', I, *Recorded Sound*, 5 (Autumn 1961), p. 150

Alexandre TANSMAN
(1897–1986)

Alexandre Tansman was born at Lódź in Poland and studied music at Warsaw University. In 1919 he emigrated to Paris, where he has lived ever since, apart from the years 1941–6 which he spent in the USA. Ravel befriended him on his arrival in Paris and introduced him to his publisher, Jacques Durand. Tansman has composed prolifically, including orchestral works, film scores and music for guitar.

Boléro was first performed as a ballet by Ida Rubinstein, commissioned by her, and it was not a musical success. And then Toscanini came with the New York Philharmonic and played it much faster. And Ravel was not pleased at all. We were in the same box and he wouldn't stand up when Toscanini tried to get him to take a bow. Then he went backstage and told Toscanini, 'It's too fast,' and Toscanini said, 'It's the only way to save the work.'

Alexandre Tansman
in conversation with the editor

René CHALUPT

The décor (of *Boléro*), by Alexandre Benois, represented a hovel in the Paralelo: on a platform in the middle of a large room a woman danced, while all around her was a throng of men inflamed by desire at the sight. Ravel accepted this interpretation of *Boléro* but it was not what he had in mind. To begin with, he saw the work not between four walls but in the open air. He wanted to emphasize the Arab element in the persistent repetition of the two themes. Then he discovered an analogy between the alternation of the two themes welded together like the links of a chain, and a factory assembly line. For that, room had to be found in the décor for a factory so that a group of male and female workers could come out of their workshops and join in the dance of the crowd. Finally, he wanted to evoke memories of bull-fighting by introducing a clandestine idyll between Marilena and a *torero*; the jealous lover could then arrive unexpectedly and stab the *torero* under Marilena's balcony.

René Chalupt
Ravel au miroir de ses lettres (Paris, 1956) pp. 237–8

Arthur Honegger

Arthur HONEGGER (1892–1955)

Arthur Honegger was born in Le Havre of Swiss parents. He studied at the Paris Conservatoire and was then grouped in 1920 with Darius Milhaud, Francis Poulenc, Georges Auric, Germaine Tailleferre and Louis Durey as a member of 'Les Six'. Honegger and Ravel always had a great regard for each other.

> Ravel said to me, in that serious, objective manner which was characteristic of him: 'I've written only one master-piece – *Boléro*. Unfortunately, there's no music in it.'

Arthur Honegger
Incantation aux fossiles (Lausanne, 1948), pp. 91–2

Edmond MAURAT
(1881–1972)

Edmond Maurat was a student of Gedalge and Widor. For more than thirty years he was director of the conservatory of music at Saint-Etienne.

I was having lunch in Marseilles one day with the conductor Paul Paray and he remembered taking Ravel to the casino at Monte-Carlo. As they went through the gaming room, Paray asked him if he would like a go. Ravel replied: 'I wrote *Boléro* and won. I'll stick there.'

Edmond Maurat
Souvenirs musicaux et littéraires (Saint-Etienne, 1977), p. 127

V

On composing

At work

Ravel really preferred not to talk about the way he composed – it was a private process and none of anybody else's business. But pupils and friends were sometimes rewarded by candour:

Edmond MAURAT

Mme André Bloch tells me of the curious conversation she had in the summer with Ravel. She wanted to know how he composed, how he sketched out his works, how ideas came to him and how he put them to good use. Ravel did not try and evade the question but met it head on, saying:

'I don't have ideas. To begin with, nothing forces itself on me.'

'But if there's no beginning, how do you follow it up? What do you write down first of all?'

'A note at random, then a second one and, sometimes, a third. I then see what results I get by contrasting, combining and separating them. From these various experiments there are always conclusions to be drawn; I explore the contents and developments of these. These half-formed ideas are built up automatically; I then range and order them like a mason building a wall. As you see, there's nothing mysterious or secret in all this.'

Edmond Maurat
Souvenirs musicaux et littéraires (Saint-Etienne, 1977), p. 128

COLETTE
(1873–1954)

Colette (Sidonie-Gabrielle Colette) had a full life as a music-hall star, actress and writer. She is perhaps best remembered for her *Claudine* novels, written at the instigation of her first husband, the critic Willy (Henri Gauthier-Villars).

It was in Mme de Saint-Marceaux's salon that I met Ravel for the first time. He was young, too young to have yet become simple. He wore side-whiskers and all his hair emphasized the contrast between his striking head and his tiny body. He liked loud ties and frilly shirts. He wanted to be noticed but at the same time was afraid of the critics; and Willy was cruel to him. Perhaps he was really shy, but he remained distant and reserved.

Years later M. Rouché[1] asked me to write the scenario for a fantasy-ballet at the Opéra. Being a slow, laborious worker, I still do not know how I produced *L'Enfant et les sortilèges* for him in eight days . . . He liked it and began to suggest some composers. I considered them as politely as I could. Then after a silence Rouché said, 'And if I suggested Ravel?' I stopped being polite instantly and gave vent to my enthusiasm. 'We mustn't be under any illusions,' Rouché said, 'it could take a long time, even if Ravel accepts.'

He accepted. It did take a long time. He took away my libretto and we had no more news of Ravel or of *L'Enfant*. Where was he working? *Was* he working? Then the war came and total silence descended. I stopped thinking about *L'Enfant et les sortilèges*.

Five years went by and suddenly the completed work and its composer emerged from the silence. But Ravel did not treat me as any sort of privileged person, he gave me no commentary on the work or any preliminary hearing of it, even of fragments. The only thing he seemed to be worried about was the miaowing duet between the two cats, and he asked me most seriously if I

---

[1] The director of the Paris Opéra from 1914 to 1944.

Colette

would mind his changing 'mouaô' into 'mouain' – or perhaps it was the other way round . . .

The years had removed, along with the frilly shirts and the side-whiskers, his small man's haughtiness. His hair, now a mixture of white and black, crowned him with a sort of plumage and while he was talking he would fold his delicate, rodent's hands and his gaze would flit over the surface of things like a squirrel's.

The score of *L'Enfant et les sortilèges* is now famous. How can I describe my emotion when, for the first time, I heard the little drum accompanying the shepherd's procession? The moonlight in the garden, the flight of the dragonflies and bats . . . 'Isn't it fun?' Ravel would say. But I could feel a knot of tears tightening in my throat.

Colette
Maurice Ravel par quelques-uns de ses familiers (Paris, 1939), pp. 119–22

Hélène JOURDAN-MORHANGE

At Fez, M. Boris Masslow, the Director of Fine Arts, was showing Ravel round the Embassy and its wonderful gardens.

'*Cher maître*,' he said, 'what a setting to inspire you to write something Arabian!'

To which Ravel replied briskly,

'If I wrote something Arabian, it would be much more Arabian than all this!'

For a number of years Ravel had talked to his friends continually about his projected opera *Jeanne d'Arc* on the novel by Delteil[1]. The music was never written but

---

[1] Joseph Delteil (1894–1977).

the outline was mapped out. When I told him I was surprised that Delteil's novel could really satisfy his refined tastes, he said, 'Exactly, I want to bring out Jeanne's peasant simplicity and her brutal, warlike side.' He was to write the libretto himself, 'and Delteil is an inspiration for the *images d'Epinal*[2] aspect of my opera-oratorio.' He imagined the crowds, like ancient choruses, massed in triangles on either side of the stage and commenting on the action. The film *Metropolis*[3], the hit of the time, had impressed him by its new way of presenting the movements of massed humanity.

Ravel would have liked to demonstrate the opposition between Jeanne as a child and Jeanne as a soldier and even spoke of having two performers for the two roles. The idea of having, during the attack on Orleans, the distant strains of *Tipperary* on the English side and the *Marseillaise* and the *Madelon* on the French one appealed to his penchant for mystification: anachronisms in the manner of Bernard Shaw, whose *Saint Joan* had moved Ravel very much – indeed, I got the impression that the spirit of Shaw was slowly supplanting that of Delteil. The musical tableaux Ravel had in mind were on these lines:

Jeanne with her sheep – the Court – Meeting with the King – Siege of Orleans – Capture of Orleans – Arraignment before the French Priests and the British Functionaries (sarcastic music, Ravel said) – then The Stake – Jeanne's Death – Entry into Heaven.

One of Ravel's firmest intentions was not to bring the Eternal Father on to the stage ('There's no way I can encumber Him with a long beard,' he said with a laugh) and he had decided that Jeanne would be on the right of Christ, who 'had not noticed the criminal activity

---

[2] Epinal, in Vosges, famous from the mid-eighteenth century for *images,* sheets of little coloured pictures illustrating legends, Bible stories, historical and contemporary events or life in foreign lands.

[3] Fritz Lang's Expressionist view of the future, first shown in 1926.

on earth'. Luminous rays would have indicated that Jeanne was in heaven, while trumpets *à la* Fra Angelico announced her arrival.

Ravel dreamed of writing a 'grand opera' in the manner of Meyerbeer (his latest enthusiasm). That is all we know, because even if Ravel the librettist let slip one or two confidences, Ravel the composer never spoke a word of his activities. But, scrupulous craftsman that he was, he reckoned that he would need ten years to finish the work.

Hélène Jourdan-Morhange
Ravel et nous (Geneva, 1945), pp. 227–8, 235–7

Vlado PERLEMUTER
(born 1904)

Vlado Perlemuter studied with Alfred Cortot at the Paris Conservatoire and in 1921 won the Prix Diémer, against competition from winners of the First Prize for piano over the previous ten years. He later returned to the Conservatoire as Professor of Piano. In the late 1920s he studied Ravel's piano works with the composer.

When I was working on 'Scarbo' with Ravel, he said to me, 'I wanted to produce a caricature of romanticism'. But he added under his breath, 'Maybe I got carried away'. He also said, with a slight air of mockery, 'I wanted to write an orchestral transcription for piano'.

Vlado Perlemuter (with Hélène Jourdan-Morhange)
Ravel d'après Ravel (Lausanne, 1957), pp. 36, 38

Robert de FRAGNY

'The G major Concerto took two years of work, you
know. The opening theme came to me on a train between
Oxford and London. But the initial idea is nothing. The
work of chiselling then began. We've gone past the days
when the composer was thought of as being struck by
inspiration, feverishly scribbling down his thoughts on a
scrap of paper. Writing music is seventy-five per cent an
intellectual activity. This effort is often more pleasant for
me than having a rest.'

Conversation with Ravel, recalled by Robert de Fragny
Echo liberté, 7 November 1950

Manuel ROSENTHAL

The first time I went to see him after he became ill, there
were some manuscripts lying on the piano and I asked his
permission to look at them. He said sadly, 'Oh well, now
you can, because I'm not going to go on with that
composition'. And to my astonishment I could see that it
looked like any composition by Bach or Mozart: a
melodic line with a figured bass, and only when he
couldn't figure the chords he'd had to write them out.
But it was very simple, written on two or three staves, no
more.

Once when I came for my lesson I saw the fire burning.
Among the ashes I could see still a piece of manuscript
paper. I asked him what it was. 'That's a good lesson for
you,' he said. 'Sometimes you think I'm too harsh with
you, too stern, too critical. Well, I have just destroyed

the finale of the Sonata for violin and piano. You know it, I've shown it to you.' I said, 'But the finale was really charming, a wonderful piece of music.' He said, 'I know. I liked it very much. But it didn't fit the sonata. It was not the right kind of finale for the first and second movements. So I have destroyed it and composed another finale which is not so good, but it's a good finale.'

La Valse has two things in it. One is a tribute to the genius of Johann Strauss. Ravel thought that the waltz was a form which had always puzzled composers. He claimed that all composers really had the desire to succeed in writing a very good waltz. In fact he reminded me of the anecdote about Brahms in a salon – the young girl asking him to write something in an autograph album and Brahms drawing a stave and putting on it in the first notes of *The Blue Danube* and underneath it the words 'Alas, not by Johannes Brahms'. Ravel said, 'You see, we all try to write a waltz as good as that. Unfortunately it's very difficult. Therefore I have tried to write a symphonic waltz as a tribute to the genius of Johann Strauss.' The other thing we find in *La Valse* is at the end – and long before the end, from the start of the second half – a kind of anguish, a very dramatic feeling of death. Instead of ending merely brilliantly, it ends brilliantly but with a sort of cry from the whole orchestra. I think that in the later part of his life many of Ravel's compositions show that he had a feeling for a dramatic death – the *Boléro*, for instance.

Physically, I could say, personally, Ravel hated revolution. I asked him once if he could tell me the difference between evolution and revolution . . . He said, 'Suppose that you are in a room, studying . . . ; after a few hours you feel that the atmosphere is a little stuffy and you need to change the air, and you open the window. You let the fresh air enter the room, after a while you close the window, that's all. That's evolution. You are in the room and you feel that you need a change of air, and you take a stone, put that through the window and break the window. Of course the fresh air enters, but after that you have to repair the window. That's revolution.' And he said, 'I don't see myself the need to break a window; I know how to open it.'

Manuel Rosenthal
in conversation with the editor

VI

As teacher

Manuel ROSENTHAL

A singer called Marcelle Gerar[1] included some of my songs in one of her recitals, and Ravel came and we met backstage after the performance. He said, 'Now we know very well that you are gifted, very gifted, but you must work very hard, because someone who is gifted has to work harder than someone who is not, and you will see how boring it is to work hard at music.' He was a very stern teacher – I cried on many occasions when I left him – and I couldn't understand at first why he was so harsh with me, being himself such a free composer and very daring. He said, 'It's for your own benefit. What you learn, you have to learn the hard way and you will thank me for it later.' And I still do . . .

One day we were studying orchestration and I asked him, 'But, *Maître*, you *never* show me a score by Debussy to study and to try and learn something from.' He said, 'But you couldn't. One can't say his music is badly orchestrated, but it's written in such a way that nobody is able to learn anything from it. Only Debussy could have written it and made it sound like only Debussy can sound.'

I had been studying with him for some time and he kept repeating, 'You still don't understand orchestration. This is only instrumentation.' Then finally I brought him a score and he said, 'Ah! Now that's orchestration.'

'But what's the difference?' I asked.

'Instrumentation,' he said, 'is when you take the music you or someone else has written and you find the right kind of instruments – one part goes to the oboe, another to the violin, another to the cello. They go along very well and the sound is good but that's all. But orchestration

See p. 131.

is when you give a feeling of the two pedals at the piano: that means that you are building an atmosphere of sound *around* the music, around the written notes – that's orchestration.'

Manuel Rosenthal
in conversation with the editor

Ralph VAUGHAN WILLIAMS (1872–1958)

Vaughan Williams was born at Down Ampney in Gloucestershire. He studied with Stanford at Cambridge and with Max Bruch in Berlin, before going to Ravel in 1908 in the hope that the French composer would bring some lightness and colour to his music. The effects of Ravel's teaching can be heard in the String Quartet no. 1 and in the song cycle *On Wenlock Edge*. The memoir that follows comes from his wife's biography of him.

Ralph wrote of his meetings and lessons with Ravel:

He was much puzzled at our first interview. When I had shown him some of my work he said that for my first lessons I had better '*écrire un petit menuet dans le style de Mozart*'. I saw at once that it was time to act promptly, so I said in my best French, 'Look here, I have given up my time, my work, my friends and my career to come here and learn from you, and I am *not* going to write a *petit menuet dans le style de Mozart*'. After that we became great friends and I learned much from him. For example, that the heavy contrapuntal Teutonic manner was not necessary. '*Complexe mais pas compliqué*' was his motto. He showed me how to orchestrate in points of colour rather than in lines. It was an invigorating experience to find all artistic problems looked at from what was to me an entirely new angle.

Brahms and Tchaikovsky he lumped together as '*tous les deux un peu lourds*'. Elgar was '*tout à fait Mendelssohn*', his own music was '*tout à fait simple, rien que Mozart*'. He was against development for its own sake – one should only develop for the sake of arriving at something better. He used to say there was an implied melodic outline in all vital music, and instanced the opening of the C minor symphony as an example of a tune which was not stated but was implicit. He was horrified that I had no pianoforte in the little hotel where I worked. *'Sans le piano on ne peut pas inventer des nouvelles harmonies.'* I practised chiefly orchestration with him. I used to score some of his own pianoforte music and bits of Rimsky and Borodin to which he introduced me for the first time.

Ralph spent three months in Paris. He was unable to find suitable rooms nearer to Ravel's home, so he continued to

Vaughan Williams

stay at l'Hôtel de l'Univers et du Portugal although it was
not particularly comfortable and the management was
rather haphazard, for there were two or three fires during
the time he was there. He enjoyed lunches and dinners in
crêmeries and cafés, but when Ravel asked him and a
publisher friend to dinner at a restaurant he felt himself
unequal to choosing the food. He excused himself as a
barbarous foreigner, and was glad he had done so when
he saw what a serious matter it was, for the preliminary
discussion lasted nearly twenty minutes. It was a splendid
meal, and the publisher ate silently throughout. After the
coffee he suddenly turned to dig Ralph in the ribs saying:
'Now we go see some jolly tarts, ha?' Ralph was surprised
and interested, but the girls were disappointing. It was
seven years since the death of Toulouse Lautrec, but the
types he had painted still persisted, a style not embraced
in Ralph's canon of beauty, and guaranteed, he said, not
to tempt any young man to lose his virtue.

Ursula Vaughan Williams
R. V. W., a Biography (London, 1964), pp. 79–81

VII

*On performances
of his music*

Marguerite LONG

One day at a dinner in the house of Mme de Saint-Marceaux, whose salon, according to Colette, was 'a citadel of artistic intimacy', Ravel said to me point-blank: 'I am composing a concerto for you. Do you mind if it ends pianissimo and with trills?' 'Of course not,' I replied, only too happy to realize the dream of all virtuosi.

One heard nothing more until 1927, the date of Ravel's journey to North America.

But after his return a year elapsed before the Concerto was put in hand – doubtless after Wittgenstein[1] had commissioned the Concerto for the left hand. Negotiations took place for a first performance of the Concerto in G in Holland, and the Concertgebouw even announced it with the composer as soloist for 9 March 1931.

But the news came that Ravel was ill and the work could not be ready. It was far from being finished and Ravel had great trouble in completing it. He told his friend Zogheb,[2] 'I can't manage to finish my Concerto, so I am resolved not to sleep for more than a second. When my work is finished I shall rest in this world . . . or in the other.'

In the meantime Ravel decided that the première of the Concerto should take place in Paris on 14 January 1932. Our Dutch friends, together with Mengelberg, who had been disappointed at all these delays, were asked to postpone their concert until the spring. They also agreed to free me from the contract to play in Amsterdam that same day.

I have said that Ravel had always wished to play his Concerto, and in much rehearsing he exhausted himself in the effort to reach virtuoso level. The long hours spent on the *Studies* of Chopin and Liszt greatly fatigued him

---

[1] Paul Wittgenstein, the Austrian pianist (the brother of the philosopher), lost his right arm in the First World War. He commissioned works also from Richard Strauss, Prokofiev and Britten.

[2] Jacques de Zogheb was a regular visitor in the last years of Ravel's life.

and deprived him of moments of fruitful inspiration. Even when this was evident he still wished to be the first to play his work and it was only when pressed by his friends – in particular Lucien Garban[1] – that he realized the difficulties confronting him in this formidable undertaking.

It can be understood how I was seized with agitation when on 11 November 1931 Ravel telephoned from Montfort l'Amaury announcing his immediate arrival with the manuscript. I had hardly composed myself when he entered holding out the precious pages. Hastily I turned to the last page to look for the pianissimo and the trills: they had become a fortissimo and percussive ninths! I realized at once how little time I had before me, not only to unravel those scrawling fly-tracks but also to keep my engagements to appear in several concerts at the end of the year.

And now, with his genius for wasting his time and that of others, Ravel harassed me unceasingly either by phone or with his visits and preventing me from practising.

It is a difficult work especially in respect of the second movement where one has no respite. I told Ravel one day how anxious I was, after all the fantasy and brilliant orchestration of the first part, to be able to maintain the cantabile of the melody on the piano alone during such a long slow flowing phrase . . . 'That flowing phrase!' Ravel cried. 'How I worked over it bar by bar! It nearly killed me!'

The day of the first performance finally arrived, and this Ravel festival was really a great musical occasion. The Salle Pleyel was full to overflowing. For a week there had not been a seat to be had and a critic of the *Paris-Soir* said: 'The composer of the *Valses nobles et sentimentales* can legitimately boast that he has given a new significance to all the folding chairs.'

Ravel conducted the *Pavane*, the *Boléro* and the Concerto. I was not very proud of the performance of that, alas!, for his conducting from a piano score was very

---

[1] Garban worked for Ravel's publisher, Durand.

uncertain. Happily all went well and the performance was adjudged a success. The third movement was encored, and I do not remember having played this work since – whether in France or abroad – without having to encore it. This doubtless constitutes an unprecedented fact in the history of Concertos. As soon as it was recognized in Paris it crossed frontiers and Ravel and I travelled far and wide in Europe. At times a programme would contain only works by Ravel, then I played the Concerto and the *Tombeau de Couperin*. At other times, when half the programme consisted of works by our friend, apart from the Concerto, I played Fauré's *Ballade*, or the *Variations symphoniques* of Franck.

We started first with Belgium: Antwerp; Liège, where we found de Freitas-Branco[1] conducting; then Brussels, where the *Tombeau* was played with orchestra. After a brief return to Paris to give the second performance of the Concerto at a Pasdeloup Concert we went to Austria.

It was then that I began to realize the legendary absent-mindedness of Ravel, whose good humour and lighthearted character were a pleasant contrast to the consequences – sometimes catastrophic – of his lack of thought and of foresight. Never did we leave Paris without his forgetting his patent leather shoes as if some malevolent Scarbo concealed them from him. He was in despair at the thought of appearing with 'boots', as he called all those which were not his favourite shoes. En route for Vienna it was naturally those that he missed first. 'You will buy some there,' I told him, but it is true that the size of his foot did not make buying a pair easy. We had to telephone Paris, and the treasure was entrusted to the guard of the next train.

It was in Bucharest that the absent-mindedness of my companion caused us our first embarrassment. Ravel had an invitation to luncheon with the King, and I with the first lady-in-waiting to the Queen, but neither of us knew, because the invitations kept their royal secret in

---

[1] Pedro de Freitas-Branco was a young Portuguese conductor who had made his début in the concert including the first performance of the G major Concerto.

the pocket of Ravel. The King with a nice simplicity and delicate appreciation of the situation himself telephoned to our hotel, and he was the first to laugh at this incident.

It was inevitable that the Concerto for the left hand would attract 'arrangers', and they were there from the very beginning. Ravel and I heard them in Vienna in the course of our European tour at the house of Paul Wittgenstein, to whom the Concerto was dedicated. He had received the score several months previously and had played it in the Austrian capital on 27 November 1931. We were invited to a grand dinner followed by a soirée. The Quartet was performed, and the host was to play the Concerto with accompaniment on a second piano, so that Ravel could at last hear his work.

I was rather anxious for, while I was seated at dinner to the right of Wittgenstein, he confided to me that he had made certain 'arrangements' in the work. Inwardly I excused him, thinking his physical disability was responsible for such liberties and I advised him to speak of it in advance to Ravel. He did not do so.

During the performance I was following the score, which I did not then know, and I could discern Ravel's face clouding over more and more at our host's misdemeanours. As soon as it was over I attempted to create a 'diversion' with the Ambassador Clauzel to avoid an incident. Alas, Ravel walked slowly over to Wittgenstein and said: 'But it is not that at all!'

In his own defence Wittgenstein said: 'I am an old hand as pianist and what you wrote does not sound right.' It was exactly the thing not to say!

'I am an old hand at orchestration and it *does* sound right,' was Ravel's answer. One can imagine the embarrassment! I remember that our friend was in such a nervous condition that he sent the ambassador's car away and we returned on foot, hoping that the severe cold would reduce his annoyance.

While admitting his right to criticize the pianist's work I could not help regretting this friction and I pleaded the case of the unfortunate Wittgenstein, who was in fact much attached to the music. But I could not convince Ravel, who in consequence of this opposed Wittgenstein's visiting Paris.

Naturally furious, the latter wrote: 'Performers must not be slaves!' And Ravel replied: 'Performers *are* slaves.'

Marguerite Long
At the Piano with Ravel (London, 1973), tr. Olive Senior-Ellis, pp. 39–45, 58–9

Hélène JOURDAN-MORHANGE

In general Ravel found that performers did not read the instructions on his scores carefully enough. I remember working on the 'Scherzo' in the *Duo*, where the rhythms and sonority of the *spiccati* must be uniform enough to pass easily from the violin to the cello. The cellist Maréchal and I went over it again and again till we were giddy. Ravel would not allow the tiniest discrepancy between the sounds of the two instruments, dissimilar though they are. So there were arguments . . .

'It's too complicated,' I said, in order to keep my end up. 'The cello has to sound like a flute and the violin like a drum. It must be great fun writing such difficult stuff but no one's going to play it except virtuosos.'

'Good!' he said, with a smile, 'then I shan't be assassinated by amateurs!'

A couple of years later he finished the *Berceuse sur le nom de Fauré* commissioned by the *Revue musicale*[1] in memory of his teacher. Do you suppose he was impressed by my interpretation? Not in the least! All his interest focused on a single note:

'How do you make that F on the E string sound as though it's on the G string?'

I could have massacred the opening of the *Berceuse* without him noticing. Each time I played it he waited for

---

[1] A monthly magazine founded by Henri Prunières in 1920.

'the' note which for him was the ultimate joy: the revelation of an unknown sonority.

Hélène Jourdan-Morhange
Ravel et nous (Geneva, 1945), pp. 180, 182–3

Jules RENARD
(1864–1910)

Jules Renard was a French writer of anti-bourgeois tendencies
whose best-known novel is *Poil de carotte*. Ravel set five of his
Histoires naturelles, sung at the first performance by Jane Bathori,
accompanied by the composer.

12 January 1907

M. Ravel, the composer of the *Histoires naturelles* (he is
dark, rich and exquisite), insists I go and hear his songs
this evening. I explained to him how ignorant I am and
asked him what he could add to my *Histoires naturelles*.

'I didn't intend to add anything,' he said, 'but to
interpret.'

'But what's the connection?'

'To say with music what you say with words when
you're gazing at a tree, for example. I think and feel in
music and I should like to think and feel the same things
as you. There is the music of instinct and feeling, which
is mine (of course, one has to learn one's technique first),
and then there is the music of the intellect, which is
d'Indy's. The hall will be full of d'Indys this evening.
They don't approve of emotion because they've no way of
explaining it. I think the opposite; but they must find me
interesting to have allowed me on to the programme.
This is a very important test for me. Anyway, I have
every confidence in my singer – she's splendid.'

Jules Renard
Journal (Paris, 1960), pp. 1100–1101

Manuel de FALLA
(1876–1946)

Manuel de Falla was beyond all doubt the greatest composer Spain has produced since the Renaissance. His relationship with Ravel was always close: although Ravel was not, like Falla, a religious believer, both men shared a belief in music's spiritual message and in the value of a small output, thoroughly considered.

I met Ravel a few days after my arrival in Paris, in the summer of 1907; this was the beginning of a heartfelt friendship. I then knew only his *Sonatine* which I had heard in Madrid and which had strongly impressed me. Some time later, when I could realize my constant desire to go to Paris and get in touch with my favourite composers, I wanted from the very first moment, to meet Ravel. This proved easy, thanks to Ricardo Viñes, brave champion of that avant-garde who had urged me to go to Paris.

Ravel and Viñes read through the *Rapsodie espagnole*, which Ravel had just published in its original piano version for four hands, and which they were to play for the first time at a concert of the *Nationale*[1]. The *Rapsodie*, besides confirming my impression of the *Sonatine*, surprised me because of its Spanish character.

But how was I to account for the subtly genuine Spanishness of Ravel, knowing, because he had told me so, that the only link he had with my country was to have been born near the border! The mystery was soon explained: Ravel's was a Spain he had felt in an idealized way through his mother. She was a lady of exquisite conversation. She spoke fluent Spanish, which I enjoyed so much when she evoked the years of her youth, spent in Madrid, an epoch certainly earlier than mine, but traces of its habits that were familiar to me still remained. Then I understood with what fascination her son must have listened to these memories that were undoubtedly

---

[1] The *Société nationale de musique,* at this time the most prestigious concert-giving body in Paris.

Manuel de Falla in Paris in the 1920s

intensified by the additional force all reminiscence gets from the song or dance theme inseparably connected with it. This explains not only the attraction exerted on Ravel, since his childhood, by a country he so frequently dreamt of, but also that later, when he wanted to characterize Spain musically, he showed a predilection for the *habanera*, the song most in vogue when his mother lived in Madrid. This was the same time that Pauline Viardot-García, famous and well acquainted with the best composers in Paris, spread the *habanera* among them. That is why that rhythm, much to the surprise of Spaniards, went on living in French music although Spain had forgotten it half a century ago.

I shall not insist on the fine sensitivity of the 'prodigious child', which glows in his melodic expressiveness – a sensitivity equally manifest in the unmistakable accents and inflexion of his lyric declamation. All I want to say is this: whoever has seen him at crucial moments of his life cannot doubt the emotional capacity of his spirit. I shall never forget how clear this became to me when his father fell critically ill. After an urgent pilgrimage through Paris we went back to his house where, realizing there was no hope, he implored me in an anguished tone to go and fetch our friend the abbé Petit to give his father the Christian sacraments. The good and quiet soul of Ravel broke out only in such circumstances, never in his music, forged in some inner world that was a refuge against an intrusive reality. How else could we explain that works like the Quartet, *Gaspard de la nuit*, and *L'Heure espagnole* had been written when their composer was going through a difficult time! I can see his extremely modest study, and feel how it contrasted with the precious quality of music that Ravel revealed to us on an old piano as modest as the whole room.

Manuel de Falla
On Music and Musicians, tr. David Urman and J. M. Thomson
(London, 1979), pp. 93–6

Henriette FAURE

Henriette Faure studied Ravel's piano works with the composer in 1922 and gave the first all-Ravel piano recital in Paris at the Théâtre des Champs-Elysées on 12 January 1923. She was seventeen years old at the time. She later made recordings of *Jeux d'eau* (the subject of the souvenir below) with the *Prélude* of 1913, and of the five *Miroirs*.

After I had played this piece, Ravel said only one thing: 'Your fountains are sad ones. Anyone would think you hadn't read the epigraph by Henri de Régnier.'[1] So I began again, this time at a livelier speed and, in the Ravelian manner, hurrying the hemidemisemiquavers leading up to some of the themes, giving a little air to the curves of the melodic lines and the gaps between them, lifting my hand abruptly to give a cleaner ending to tied notes and above all *thinking happy thoughts*, so as to turn what I had previously thought was a meditation into a sparkling divertimento. Ravel said, 'That's more like it, but you could even so be a little dreamier at the end . . . as long as . . .' and I cheekily finished his sentence with 'you don't slow down'. He might have been cross at being mimicked like that but in fact he laughed quite openly.

Henriette Faure
Mon maître Maurice Ravel (Paris, 1978), p. 95

---

[1] 'Dieu fluvial riant de l'eau qui le chatouille'. ('The river god laughing at the water as it tickles him'.)

The first page of Ravel's autograph of *Jeux d'Eau*

Charles OULMONT

One evening I sat down to play the piano for one of my mother's *soirées*, not knowing that Ravel was one of the many guests. I played, from memory of course, his *Pavane*. When I had finished the piece Ravel came up to me. I taxed him with not having warned me by some sign that he was in the audience. He ignored my complaint and, with a grimace which defies desciption, murmured:

'Listen, dear boy, remember another time that I wrote a Pavane for a dead princess.'

'But . . .'

'And not a dead Pavane for a princess.'

Charles Oulmont
ReM, Dec. 1938, p. 209

Madeleine GREY
(1897–1979)

Madeleine Grey was a French soprano, a pupil of Hettich at the Paris Conservatoire. She gave the first performance of Ravel's *Deux mélodies hébraïques* in 1920 and was his favourite interpreter of the *Chansons madécasses* which she recorded under his direction in 1932.

He was terribly demanding to work with, because his scores left nothing to chance. Some years later, in 1937, the year of his death, when he was very ill and could no longer sign his name, I had put his *Don Quichotte à Dulcinée* into my annual recital, even though it was written for a man's voice. So I wanted to have the composer's opinion and, with Poulenc as my accompanist, went to sing the three songs to him. When I had finished I asked if he had any observations to make. At first it seemed as though he did not have, but then, as though coming out of a dream, he pointed with his index finger to a bar at the end of the 'Chanson à boire' where I had made a slight rallentando *that was not in the score*. Given his condition, Poulenc and I were both astonished.

Madeleine Grey
interview for *Le Guide musical* (unpublished)

VIII

*As pianist
and conductor*

Maurice DELAGE
(1879–1961)

Maurice Delage was inspired to become a composer by hearing
Debussy's *Pelléas et Mélisande*. He was one of Ravel's few pupils.
His best-known work is the *Quatre poèmes hindous*.

Nature endowed Ravel with knotted, tapering hands and
with thumbs that could move freely round the central
joint and cover two white keys simultaneously. In *Jeux
d'eau* Ravel uses unusual fingerings to obtain the delicate
rustling of Henri de Régnier's superscription 'The river
god laughing at the water as it tickles him.' But before
that, the 'Habanera' of 1895 begins with extraordinary
appoggiaturas that fell naturally under his hands, with
the thumb of one hand playing the notes C and D
simultaneously and the other hand playing an interior
pedal C♯. An extreme example of the use of this kind of
technique is to be found in 'Scarbo', the remarkable

Ravel, Maurice and Nelly Delage and Suzanne Roland-Manuel

89

passage of twenty bars based on the movement of the thumb. The necessary agility comes from great suppleness in the wrist, the fingers held flat on the keyboard and the player sitting very low. Except in special circumstances, Ravel did not approve of pianists perched high with rounded fingers.

Maurice Delage
Maurice Ravel, incomplete lecture script in Bibliothèque Nationale (Rés. Vmb. Ms. 44)

Manuel ROSENTHAL

He used to sit very low at the piano. His hands were not above the keys but almost below them. Not only were they held flat but the palm was on a level below the keyboard, and you can see, when you look at his piano music, that there are no octave passages. On the other hand he made use of his extraordinary thumbs which were quite independent of the rest of his hand and almost on a level with his index fingers. In private, his friends used to call them 'your strangler's thumbs'. And you can see throughout his piano works the way the thumb curls under the hand to play some melody or other while the remaining fingers play the accompaniment.

Manuel Rosenthal
interview with Rémy Stricker on 'France Culture', 1985, quoted in Marcel Marnat, *Maurice Ravel* (Paris, 1986), p. 39

Gordon BRYAN

Gordon Bryan was a pianist who played in two Ravel concerts in London in 1928 and 1929, in which the composer also participated.

Before Ravel arrived, a gramophone company suggested his recording *Jeux d'eau*, but knowing about his limited technical ability from Dr Vaughan Williams, I hedged until he arrived, when he exclaimed in dismay: 'But I have never played it in my life!' His performance in the Violin and Piano Sonata, and his accompaniment to the songs, were vitally rhythmical and extremely authoritative in style, which is not always the case with composers. Even if not invariably accurate, it did not seem to matter – for instance, when he had written difficult arpeggios in the aria from *L'Heure espagnole*, which was sung by Odette de Foras, he played them 'glissando' with excellent effect.

I was turning over the music of the Violin Sonata (which was played by Frederick Holding) and during the first movement Ravel suddenly realized that he had not put on his spectacles. Whereupon he groped in his coat-tail pocket with his right hand, meanwhile attempting to play what should be on two hands with left hand alone. When he had secured the glasses, I adjusted them on his nose, to the amusement of the nearer members of the audience, but considerably less to the amusement of the violinist, who had to continue as usual during this panto-mime. Ravel was thoroughly unselfconscious, and indulged in many asides to me, commenting with self-satisfaction on the music and sundry harmonic progressions therein, as though we had been rehearsing in private.

Gordon Bryan
quoted in Norman Demuth, *Ravel* (London, 1947), pp. 175–6

Ernesto HALFFTER
(born 1905)

Ernesto Halffter was born in Madrid and studied composition with Manuel de Falla. In 1966 he became musical adviser to the Spanish Television Network.

> I remember when he came to America, he accompanied his Violin Sonata and from the musical point of view he was fantastic. He made lots of mistakes – that was because he didn't practise enough. But he gave a very good idea of what he meant. I prefer Ravel with mistakes to anyone else without them.

Ernesto Halffter
interview with Mildred Clary, 'France Culture', 1983, quoted in Marcel Marnat, *Maurice Ravel* (Paris, 1986)

> It was a moot point, sometimes discussed in a friendly way among Ravel's acquaintances, which he was worse at: playing the piano or conducting.

Paul STEFAN
(1879–1943)

Paul Stefan was a Viennese music critic and editor of the music journal *Der Anbruch*.

> The Viennese section of the ISCM had put the *Chansons madécasses* into an all-Ravel programme. He took part and accompanied Arnold Rosé[1] in the Violin Sonata, not without making some jokes about his piano technique. 'Now that's all passed off safely, I'll play you some Liszt . . .' and with humorous deliberation he struck a few

---

[1] The leader of the Rosé Quartet, which gave many performances of works by the Second Viennese School.

chords on the piano in the foyer. In the *Chansons madécasses* he simplified the piano part, saying: 'No ones's going to notice.'

Another time we had organized a little concert in his honour at the French Embassy and Ravel wanted to conduct the instrumental ensemble in the *Chansons madécasses*. All the performers were of the highest class, but they were thrown into chaos by Ravel's gesticulations. At the first rehearsal nothing was together. Then the cellist, who was in the Opera orchestra, muttered to the singer: 'We'll follow you. The *Maître* can beat time over the top of us.' So that's how it was – and the performance was perfect.

Paul Stefan
ReM, Dec. 1938, p. 278

ROLAND-MANUEL
(1891–1966)

Roland-Manuel (Alexis Manuel Lévy) was a Belgian musicologist, composer and critic. He was one of Ravel's pupils and a close friend, whose four books on Ravel and his music remain unrivalled for their insight and sympathy. He became a professor at the Schola Cantorum in Paris and an honorary professor at the Conservatoire.

Adélaïde, ou le langage des fleurs was orchestrated in fifteen days in March 1912, and appeared at Mlle Trouhanowa's *Concerts de danse* at the Châtelet the following 22 April.

Like Vincent d'Indy's *Istar*, Florent Schmitt's *Tragédie de Salomé,* and Paul Dukas' *Péri*, with which the programme was shared, *Adélaïde* was conducted by its composer. Ravel had not held a baton since the isolated performance of the Overture to *Shéhérazade*. His performance of *Adélaïde* was correct, if not masterly:

Roland-Manuel

'It isn't difficult,' he admitted the first evening, 'It's always in three-time . . .' And when we objected that the seventh waltz contained superimposed binary and ternary rhythms, he agreed that made it difficult; 'but when I get to that point, I just go round and round.'

Roland-Manuel
Maurice Ravel, tr. Cynthia Jolly (London, 1947), p. 66

Sir Henry WOOD (1869–1944)

Henry Joseph Wood was born in London and studied at the Royal Academy of Music. In 1895 he conducted the first of the Promenade Concerts and was still conducting them nearly half a century later. He was knighted in 1911.

Ravel came to London in the 1920s to conduct some of his works. On the morning in question he was to rehearse the suite *Ma Mère l'Oye*.

Exactly at ten o'clock I led him to the rostrum where he received a great welcome. He opened his score, turned several pages and then back to the first. At this he gazed for some seconds. He then turned to me in the Grand Circle.

'How many *pupitres* (desks) of first violins are there?'
'Eight, sir.'
A long silence. Then (very slowly): 'I will take only five *pupitres*.'
Ravel turned over more pages. 'How many *pupitres* are there of second violins?'
'Eight, sir.'
'I will take only five *pupitres*.'
This went on for some time because he asked the same question about the violas, cellos and basses. The orchestra

Sir Henry Wood

behaved like angels; not a muscle was moved, not a sound uttered. *But the first note they played was at 10.23 by my watch!* And, I may add, I had a concerto and a symphony to rehearse.

Sir Henry J. Wood
My Life of Music (London, 1938), pp. 129–30

Whether through the excellence of American orchestras or the kindness of American audiences, Ravel's tour of the USA during the first four months of 1928 was a resounding success:

Alexandre TANSMAN

I would say people in Europe didn't know the real Ravel. I had the good fortune to make my first tour of the United States at the same time as Ravel. At the first concert, for instance, in New York with the Boston Symphony and Koussevitsky conducting, when the audience stood up to applaud he had tears in his eyes. He said to me, 'It wouldn't happen to me in Europe.'

He was not a good conductor. I went to his second concert in Boston and he conducted his *Rapsodie espagnole* and he was not at home at all. Fortunately they had played it already with Koussevitsky. But he didn't realize. When I went backstage he said, 'I'm sorry you didn't come yesterday, it was better still.'

Alexandre Tansman,
in conversation with the editor

René CHALUPT

Ravel was conducting in Biarritz when, just before going out on to the platform, he realized that he had lost or forgotten the handkerchief to go in his top pocket. Robert Casadesus[1] offered to lend him his but Ravel, meticulous as ever, refused on the grounds that the pianist's initials were not the same as his own.

René Chalupt
Ravel au miroir de ses lettres (Paris, 1956), p. 241

---

[1] The well-known French pianist, who made a recording of all Ravel's piano works. See p. 109

IX

Fellow artists

Manuel ROSENTHAL

One day during the last months of his life he looked very sad and as a kind of joke (a very bad joke, I have to say) I said to him, '*Maître*, supposing that you were preparing a musical programme for your funeral, what would you like to be played?' And immediately he said, '*L'Après-midi d'un faune*'. I said, 'What a strange choice for a funeral!' He said, 'You know, it's because it's the only score ever written that is absolutely perfect.'

Manuel Rosenthal
In conversation with the editor

ROLAND-MANUEL

Ravel knew Debussy personally, and at the beginning their relationship was excellent. Although they were never intimate friends, they were at least good friends for a great many years. Because it gave him pleasure, and because he wished to pay homage to a man of genius, Ravel transcribed for two pianos the *Prélude à l'après-midi d'un faune*, a work which he himself never tired of calling a masterpiece. 'He knew and sincerely admired Debussy,' wrote Louis Laloy[1] in *La Musique retrouvée*. 'I did everything in my power to prevent a break between them, but too many stupid meddlers seemed to take pleasure in making it inevitable, by sacrificing, for example, Debussy's Quartet on the altar of Ravel's, or by raising absurd questions about the priority of the *Habanera* and the second of the *Estampes*. The two composers then stopped visiting each other; and as their respect for each other was entirely mutual, I can vouch for the fact that they both regretted the rupture.'

---

[1] Debussy's first biographer and later secretary of the Paris Opéra.

Not so much to invalidate the evidence of an accredited Debussyist, as to preserve a piece of enlightened commentary, I wrote down in 1912 the following utterance by the composer of the *Valses nobles et sentimentales*: 'It's probably better for us, after all, to be on frigid terms for illogical reasons.' All the same, the two composers kept up a social and artistic relationship up to 1902, at a time when Debussy's genius, which had arrived at maturity, was burning with its brightest flame and revealing its most engaging charm. Then, and only then, in Ravel's work could there be seen, in the String Quartet and the three *Shéhérazade* songs faint, but unmistakable, traces of Debussy's influence.

'My String Quartet,' said Ravel, 'represents a conception of musical construction, imperfectly realized no doubt, but set out much more precisely than in my earlier compositions.'

All the same, though not to contradict the composer, it is noticeable how, if this work really represents so absolute a conception of structure, it does so with extraordinary vigour, rhythmical ease and melodic verve. The intense suavity of this grave, youthful music makes it appear the most spontaneous work Ravel has ever written. The outbursts of lyricism find forceful expression within the framework of an uncompromising classicism without breaking it; they move so freely within it that the composer sometimes used to doubt his success. The more the secret powers which governed him unawares attracted him, the more he mistrusted them. He was suspicious of the lure of spontaneity which had led him so easily from the arbitrary to the necessary, to borrow a happy phrase from Paul Valéry. Contrary to his practice, he submitted his work to the judgement of his friends, and the criticism of the master to who it was dedicated. Fauré did not mince matters. He found the fourth movement stunted, badly balanced, in fact, a failure. In the end, Debussy was asked for his opinion, and he reassured and congratulated the younger man, writing him a solemn injunction: 'In the name of the gods of music, and in mine, do not touch a single note of what you have written in your Quartet.'

Roland-Manuel
Maurice Ravel, tr. Cynthia Jolly (London, 1947), pp. 35–6

Hélène JOURDAN-MORHANGE

All through his life Ravel used to tell a story about how he took his String Quartet into Fauré's class and how Fauré received it with less than his usual enthusiasm; indeed he pulled a face and thought it was no good. Some days later he asked Ravel to bring the manuscript back again:

'Why do you want to see it, *cher maître*,' said Ravel, 'since it's rubbish?'

'I could have been wrong,' Fauré replied.

Ravel attached an enormous importance to this simple little story.

Ravel always defended Saint-Saëns's music against his detractors: 'It's finely put together, which is not negligible. Nothing is better written than his piano concertos and young composers will always have a lot to learn from his orchestration.' And he added: 'He composes within an architectural order.' In the case of Paul Dukas, he admired the integrity of the man as much as that of the composer; he thought *The Sorcerer's Apprentice* was a complete success. He considered Fauré as the master of French song but, as young composers were later to do from him, he broke away quite early from an influence which might have retarded his own development, and Fauré approved of this. In spite of the divergence in aesthetic between his music and that of Florent Schmitt, he was full of praise for Schmitt's expertise and recognized him as a powerful musical force. Roussel was too close to him to be discussed, but he appreciated the fine musicianship in Jacques Ibert's operetta *Angélique*.

Weber was one of his really favourite composers, and his admiration went on growing to the end of his life. How many times have I heard him extolling the merits of *Der Freischütz*? The final quintet in particular bowled him over and he used to speak of it like a gourmet savouring the memory of a succulent dish. He considered Weber as a great precursor and was astonished that his *lieder* were not sung more often:

'No more fruitful source,' he used to explain to me, 'fed German romanticism. At a time when the Italian style was invading music, Weber kept it at bay by discoveries which one could compare to Goethe's, finding in popular music the freshness which gave his *lieder* a new form: the inner feeling, the drama, if you like, became the stuff of the music.' He used to claim that, without Weber, Wagner would not perhaps have achieved the intimate communion between text and music.

On the question of orchestration, Ravel always said how much he had learnt from reading the scores of Rimsky-Korsakov and Strauss. 'Strauss,' he used to say, 'is the liberator who has been able to extend the liberties taken by Berlioz, and he has given the wind instruments a new importance, new at least for the time when he was writing' – and Ravel used to cite *Till Eulenspiegel* (1895) as the work of a real humorist. He would also say, despite his total admiration for Strauss's skill as an orchestrator: 'It's only his irresistible comic sense which sometimes saves his tunes from an excessively facile sentimentality.'

After the première of Georges Auric's ballet *Les Matelots*, given by the Ballets Russes in 1925, Ravel, who liked the work very much, wanted to go and congratulate the composer.

'What?' I said, 'go and congratulate Auric after the unflattering article he's just written about you?'

'Why not?' Ravel replied, looking me straight in the eye. 'I like his ballet. So he knocks Ravel? Well, quite right too; if he didn't knock Ravel he'd be writing Ravel, and there's quite enough of that!'

I was with Ravel at one of the Paris performances of Schoenberg's *Pierrot lunaire*. He had said to me, 'You're going to hear an exceptional work. Schoenberg is the greatest composer in Austria and his disciples in Vienna adore him . . . it'll be a revelation.' I must confess there was no revelation for me that evening and, in short, I quarrelled with Ravel, interested as he always was in the discoveries of others. But I had my reward. Some years later Ravel confessed that in fact I had not been completely wrong: Schoenberg was certainly a great man, but all those procedures and that deliberate intellectualism ran the risk of becoming as academic as any other music based on theories. 'All theory is grey,' he said, 'but the precious tree of life is green.'[1]

Hélène Jourdan-Morhange
Ravel et nous (Geneva, 1945), pp. 56, 77–8, 81, 89, 98–9, 102–4

Alfredo CASELLA
(1883–1947)

Alfredo Casella was born in Turin and came to Paris in 1896 to study piano with Diémer and composition with Fauré. He played the piano part in the first performance of Ravel's Piano Trio in 1915. He was among the most important Italian composers of his time.

Even the most uncompromising foes were ultimately compelled to acknowledge his technical mastery and his sense of form. His music, for technical perfection, ranks with Bach's, Mozart's, and Chopin's. His mentality was fundamentally scholastic – an idiosyncrasy betrayed by his fondness for contrapuntal artifices such as fugue, stretti, inversions, canons, and so on. His inclination to start from some musical model – to place himself in front of a Mozart sonata or a Saint-Saëns concerto as a painter

---

[1] Words spoken by Mephistopheles in Goethe's *Faust*.

in front of a landscape or a sitter – has often been mentioned. The wonder is that the outcome was always thoroughly original and unlike the model.

He composed for the élite around him, never believing that there could be two kinds of music – one for the upper classes and another for the proletarians. The last time I saw him, three years ago, as I was alluding to the popularity of his works, he said to me: 'Well, we must not exaggerate: but if instead of nourishing the masses on old commonplaces one attempted to foster in them a sense for true music, they would respond.' I never heard him judge a brother composer unfairly. Contrary to most composers, he was a keen admirer of talent wherever he found it; and his mind was as free from jealousy as it was cultured and alert.

Alfredo Casella
in *Musica d'oggi*, March 1938, quoted in *Musical Times*, July 1938

'SPECULUM'

He spoke little of his own music, but a good deal of that of others – and not in order to run it down, as is usually the case. He was interested in Casella's, Pizzetti's, and Malipiero's, and also in that of the younger Frenchmen and notably 'The Six', among whom it was the fashion to regard him as old-fashioned and jaundiced (later under Cocteau's influence their attitude to him changed). Naturally enough, he had but little appreciation for their two most obvious qualities: facility and speed. He saw them turning out, in a twelvemonth or less, two or three string quartets, sonatas, and sonatinas, symphonies and sinfoniettas, concertos and concertinos, and heard everybody around him praising them for their gift of the gab, the triteness of their melodies, their contempt of adjustment and polish. It seemed, he said, as though they never could muster courage to scrap a single bar of their works. His own methods, of course, were the very reverse.

'Speculum'
in *Rassegna musicale*, January 1938, quoted in *Musical Times*, July 1938.

Ravel played little part in the 'official' musical life of France, but he did agree from time to time to sit on juries, for the Paris Conservatoire and other institutions.

Edward J. DENT
(1876–1957)

Edward Dent was a musicologist, opera translator, and for many years Professor of Music at Cambridge University.

Ravel was limited in his sympathies by the Frenchness of his genius. When he was on the jury of the ISCM in Geneva in December 1928, I remember very well how little part he played in our deliberations, despite his personal charm and idealistic outlook. When it came to voting it was hard to get him to commit himself and some of the scores baffled him completely. Heinz Tiessen was praising a new symphony by a young German composer. 'It's all Chinese to me,' said Ravel, 'but if you tell me it's good German music I'll vote for it.'

Professor E. J. Dent
ReM, Dec. 1938, p. 237

But Ravel was not entirely isolationist in his outlook:

Alexandre TANSMAN

Ravel once said to me, 'A composer who shows no influences should change his profession.'

Alexandre Tansman
in conversation with the editor

Frank MARTIN
(1890–1974)

Frank Martin was born in Geneva and studied there at the Jacques-Dalcroze Institute, where he was appointed professor in 1928. His best-known work is probably the *Petite symphonie concertante* of 1945.

I met Ravel only once, at a sitting of a festival jury. In the course of our conversation he said: 'The greatest of all dangers for an artist is sincerity. Had we been sincere we should have written nothing but Wagnerian music.' It seems to me that he was referring not to his generation, but to himself alone. Maybe, in his youth, at a time when he had as yet no clear vision of his own style to be, he saw in Wagner's music an ideal example of resourcefulness and power of expression, of fully satisfying beauty. Under the impulsion of that sincerity of which he was speaking, he, or any other young composer, might have been lured into aiming at composing similarly beautiful music. But the true artist is primarily concerned with seeking not only his own self, but also the true expression of it. The 'dangerous' sincerity, in Ravel's mind, was that which induces the artist to follow his taste of the moment, to resort to the means of expression that appeal to him in the music of others. He had the courage to resist the impulses that might have made him untrue to his own nature, and to obey the dictates of a more deeply rooted impulse. By so doing he may have deprived himself of the possibility of composing the big-scale works he was dreaming of: but probably he achieved an art that, owing to its supreme perfection, has an extraordinarily convincing quality.

Frank Martin
in *Schweizerische Musikzeitung,* 15 March 1938, quoted in *Musical Times*, July 1938.

Gaby CASADESUS
(born 1901)

Gaby Casadesus was born in Marseilles and studied at the Paris Conservatoire with Louis Diémer. In 1921 she married Robert Casadesus and they gave many recitals both together and separately over the next fifty years.

Gaby and Robert Casadesus

My husband already loved Mozart but he thought the Beethoven quartets were the most outstanding *chef-d'oeuvres* in the world. Ravel liked the Beethoven quartets, but he said, 'If you look at the Mozart quartets they are much more interesting than the Beethoven. And the concertos . . . you have only five concertos by Beethoven, but look how many you have by Mozart.' Chopin also was a god for Ravel. Ravel used to say of the *Tarantella*, which is usually thought to be a cheap piece of Chopin, 'You ought to play it, not just for the Tarantella itself but for the beautiful chord at the end.'

Gaby Casadesus
in conversation with the editor

Manuel ROSENTHAL

One day he was speaking to me in glowing terms about Puccini. And being the silly, impertinent young man I was, I started to sneer. At that Ravel flew into a towering rage, locked us both into his little studio at Montfort l'Amaury and sat down at the piano. He then played me the whole of *Tosca* from memory, stopping about fifty times on the way to ask, 'Have you anything to complain of about that passage? Look how good the harmony is, how he respects the form, what a clever, original and interesting modulation there is in that tune.' Finally he took down the score to show me how perfect the orchestration is. He said, 'This is exactly what I did with *Le Tombeau de Couperin:* this economy of means by which two solo instruments in Puccini's orchestra produce such an impact – that is the mark of a great artist.'

Manuel Rosenthal
interview with Rémy Stricker, 'France Culture', quoted in Marcel Marnat, *Maurice Ravel* (Paris, 1986), p. 145

Nils GREVILLIUS
(1893–1970)

Nils Grevillius was conductor of the Royal Orchestra of Stockholm from 1924 to 1953.

I first met Ravel in 1920 in Paris, where I was going to conduct a concert. I asked his opinion about what to put in the programme and suggested Brahms's Fourth Symphony. He actually quite liked the work, but he gave an exclamation and said:

'But, Monsieur, you can't play that awful waltz in Paris . . .'

'What do you mean?' I replied in some surprise. 'Brahms's Fourth Symphony is not a waltz.'

'Oh no?' said he roguishly, and began to hum:

Nils Grevillius
ReM, Dec. 1938, p. 268

Igor STRAVINSKY
(1882–1971)

Igor Stravinsky was born near St Petersburg and studied composition with Rimsky-Korsakov. He came to Paris first in 1910 for the performances of *The Firebird* by Diaghilev's Ballets Russes. Diaghilev then commissioned him and Ravel together to produce a performing version of Mussorgsky's opera *Khovanshchina*. In the 1920s Ravel's failure to appreciate works like *Mavra* and *Les Noces* led to a coolness between the two men.

Stravinsky

Ravel came to Clarens to live with me and we worked together there in March–April 1913. At that same time also, I composed my *Three Japanese Lyrics* and Ravel his *Trois poèmes de Mallarmé* which I still prefer to any music of his. I remember an excursion I made with Ravel from Clarens to Varèse, near Lago Maggiore, to buy Varese paper. The town was very crowded and we could not find two hotel rooms or even two beds, so we slept together in one.

Ravel? When I think of him, for example in relation to Satie, he appears quite ordinary. His musical judgement was very acute, however, and I would say that he was the only musician who immediately understood *Le Sacre du printemps*. He was dry and reserved and sometimes little darts were hidden in his remarks, but he was always a very good friend to me. He drove a truck or ambulance in the war, as you know, and I admired him for it because at his age and with his name he could have had an easier place – or done nothing. He looked rather pathetic in his uniform; so small, he was two or three inches smaller than I am.

Stravinsky
Conversations with Igor Stravinsky, Igor Stravinsky and Robert Craft (London, 1959), p. 62

Jean COCTEAU
(1889–1963)

Jean Cocteau was born in Paris and played a part in most of that city's cultural movements as artist, designer, writer, critic and film-maker.

I remember taking Ravel to the Châtelet Theatre two days before the première of *Parade*.[1] The orchestra was rehearsing and threatening to go on strike on the grounds that they were being asked to play 'casino music'. Ravel listened, with his birdlike head on one shoulder, and

---

[1] This took place on 18 May 1917.

then, fixing me with a firm gaze, admitted to me he did
not understand the mechanism of music which, he said,
was not bathed in any sonorous fluid.

Jean Cocteau
ReM, Dec. 1938, pp. 204–5

Darius MILHAUD
(1892–1974)

Darius Milhaud was born at Aix-en-Provence and entered the Paris
Conservatoire in 1909. In 1916 he went to Brazil and shortly after his
return became a member of 'Les Six'. He managed to remain on
friendly terms with both Ravel and Satie. Although Ravel was
occasionally tart about Milhaud's prolific output, he admired much
of his music and especially his opera *Les Malheurs d'Orphée* of 1924.

I remember once Ravel came to have lunch at my house
very soon after the first performance of Satie's *Socrate*,[1]
which I adored. And he didn't like it at all – he didn't
understand it, that's all. And he told me that he could
never agree with a work which for him was so poor – in
invention, poor in everything. This sort of very pure line
and very simple harmonies are far removed from the
Ravelian aesthetic.

When the first performance of *La Valse* was given, I
was a critic for one of the newspapers and I remember I
wrote a very impertinent review (with all the im-
pertinence that young people can have and *must* have)
and said it was 'Saint-Saëns for the Russian ballet'. I still
think it is! I suppose Ravel was a little shocked by this
statement, but he never showed it. When the Group of
Six was formed after the war, then Ravel was one of the
composers we criticized the most. I must say he was
extremely fair, because when he was asked by critics
what he thought of the younger generation he was very
generous and always spoke of my work very nicely, and it

---

[1] The first performance with orchestra was given on 7 June 1920.

Darius Milhaud, Jean Cocteau and Francis Poulenc

was almost a little embarrassing for me because I couldn't give him back this nice appreciation.

Darius Milhaud
BBC interview, 24 October 1957

Francis POULENC
(1899–1963)

Francis Poulenc was born in Paris and in 1920 was one of the group of composers known as 'Les Six'. His relationship with Ravel developed into one of slightly wary respect on both sides.

I got to know Ravel, to be exact, in March 1917. At that period I was studying the piano with Ricardo Viñes and spending most of my time with him. I very much wanted to meet Ravel – I was eighteen at the time and as Ravel had been in the army and then ill, I had never met him. Viñes said, 'Listen, the best thing would be . . . I'll ask him to see you', Ravel being a close friend of his. 'You can go and see him one morning, show him your music and play him the *Sonatine*, since you want to.'

I remember . . . I wanted to play him the 'Forlane', 'Menuet' and 'Rigaudon' from *Le Tombeau de Couperin* as well. That's to say, I 'was' to have played but he stopped me after three minutes. Maybe he didn't like my playing, but anyway the conversation turned to composition. I showed him some feeble piano pieces of mine, which he criticized severely but kindly, and then we talked of more general matters.

Ravel was paradox incarnate and, when he was with a young composer, he emphasized, I think, his paradoxical attitude. I learnt therefore that Schumann (here some derisive puffing) was very ordinary; that Mendelssohn was marvellous and his *Songs without Words* a thousand times better than Schumann's *Carnaval*; that all Debussy's late works, which I adored and was one of the few who did – that's to say *Jeux* and the piano *Etudes* – all that was not 'good' Debussy; that, from the musical point of view, Debussy's old age was unproductive, that Saint-Saëns was a composer of genius and that Chabrier's orchestration didn't fit his music, etc. etc. I was dumb-founded and left him in a state of shock. He wasn't at all the sort of composer I'd expected, and this meeting explains why, when later on Satie said (and here I must use a rude word): 'That arse Ravel, he talks a load of rubbish!', I then naturally followed the Satie-Auric line, that's to say firmly anti-Ravel.

You know that Stravinsky and Ravel had been very close and that in 1913 Ravel lived for a time near Stravinsky in Switzerland while he was reorchestrating lost passages of Mussorgsky's opera *Khovanshchina* for Diaghilev. Then, after that, there was a great coolness between them which lasted until Ravel's death. Ravel was very honest with himself and equally intransigent with others, and from *Les Noces* onwards he didn't like Stravinsky's music any more: he didn't like *Oedipus Rex* or anything of that sort, and so they never ever saw each other. I was present at an extraordinary and historic scene in the apartment of Misia Sert, who knew everybody and was Diaghilev's guardian angel, when Ravel introduced *La Valse* to Diaghilev. There weren't many people there – Diaghilev, Massine, Stravinsky, two or three of Diaghilev's secretaries, myself and Marcelle Meyer. Ravel came and played *La Valse* for Diaghilev on the piano. Diaghilev was to put *La Valse* on with the Ballets Russes and Misia's husband, José-Maria Sert, was to be the designer.

Ravel arrived very simply, with his music under his arm, and Diaghilev said to him, in that nasal voice of his: 'Well now, my dear Ravel, how lucky we are to be hearing *La Valse*.' And Ravel played *La Valse* with Marcelle Meyer, not very well maybe, but anyway it was Ravel's *La Valse*. Now at the time I knew Diaghilev very well . . . and I saw the false teeth begin to move, then the monocle, I saw he was embarrassed, I saw he didn't like it and was going to say 'No'. When Ravel had got to the end, Diaghilev said something which I think is very true. He said 'Ravel, it's a masterpiece . . . but it's not a ballet . . . It's the portrait of a ballet . . . It's the painting of a ballet.' And I think that's the reason why no one has ever choreographed *La Valse* successfully. But the extraordinary thing was, Stravinsky said *not a word*!

That was in 1921.[1] I was twenty-two and, as you can imagine, absolutely flabbergasted. Ravel proceeded to give me a lesson in modesty which has lasted me all my life: he picked up his music quite quietly and, without worrying about what we all thought of it, calmly left the room.

One of the last times he conducted in public was at the Châtelet Theatre, conducting the *Rapsodie espagnole* at the Colonne concerts. The *Rapsodie* had survived through my anti-Ravel period and I told him how, each time I heard it, I thought it was such a marvellous work.

'The *Rapsodie espagnole*, yes, yes,' he said, 'but the "Habanera" is a flop!'

'I know why you say that,' I replied, 'it's because it was originally a piece for two pianos which you inserted into the *Rapsodie* and orchestrated.'

'No, no,' he insisted, 'I like the music, but it's so badly orchestrated!'

'How can you possibly claim that?' I protested.

And then he said something which could only have come from a truly extraordinary technician: 'The orchestra's too large for the number of bars.'

A wonderful remark. Another time he said to Auric: 'I'd like your help. I want to write an orchestration treatise like Rimsky-Korsakov's, with short extracts from my music, but to show *what should not be done . . . the things I got wrong!*' As opposed to Rimsky who offers himself as a model.

Francis Poulenc
Moi et mes amis (Paris, 1963), pp. 173–5, 177–9, 183–4

---

[1] It was in fact 1920.

X

At home

In the first months of 1921, Ravel found a small house in the village of Montfort l'Amaury, about fifty kilometres south-west of Paris. It was to remain his home until his death.

Hélène JOURDAN-MORHANGE

'Le Belvédère'! An imposing name for such a tiny house in which the objects, all to scale, looked like children's toys. All Ravel's friends knew his predilection for the Louis-Philippe style and used to bring him the most amazing knick-knacks. There was the wonderful sailing boat which, at the turn of a hidden handle, used to rock to and fro among waves of wallpaper, and the tiny sofa made of scalloped porcelain which Germaine Tailleferre discovered, and Adélaïde, the doll in a globe, made by Suzanne Roland-Manuel[1] in honour of the ballet *Adélaïde, ou le langage des fleurs*. I cannot describe here the mass of coloured boxes, glass objects, bottle-imps and 1880 bowls all over the piano, the lamps, the inkwell in the shape of a cathedral and the goose-feather on his workdesk. His last find, which every visitor had to admire, was the mechanical box on top of which perched a tiny nightingale singing the most beautiful of all the nightingale's songs: its beak would open, it wings (made of real feathers) would beat and Ravel would go into ecstasies. I never saw him tire of these bouts of admiration.

On days when work was impossible he used to go walking in the beautiful forest of Rambouillet, and there he would wander tirelessly, mulling over themes which

---

[1] The wife of Roland-Manuel; see p. 89

refused to come to life. He loved that forest and was familiar with its paths and clearings, knowing where and when a particular tree would be coming out. I often had the pleasure of going with him. In the last period of his life, despite his fatigue, he used to take me, relying on his surprisingly accurate memory, to places he had discovered years before. We covered many a kilometre to find a little plant which had delighted him by the strange red striations on its leaves, or a pond whose leaden waters gave a green reflection to the blue of the sky.

He knew all the birds and could imitate their songs and whistle their rhythms perfectly. He liked to tell a story about the war which had made a great impression on him. As a volunteer he had driven a truck in the area round Verdun and was involved in the most indescribable chaos and the most deafening uproar. The silence that followed the battle seemed to him supernatural: the fields were quiet, the sky was clear blue and suddenly, at dawn, a warbler began to sing. He was so moved by this unexpected song that he promised himself he would write a *mélodie* called 'The unconcerned warbler'. But then, with the war and his illness, he never got round to it.

All his friends used to go out to Montfort to see him, Sunday being devoted to his brother Edouard. The best time was when we met in Rambouillet of an evening to drink aperitifs and gossip. During the week Ravel sometimes used to work for several nights on end. When he was writing his Sonata for violin and piano he would often ask me to come over to put in fingerings and bowings. Everything to do with technique interested him and he wanted to know the violin's most extreme capabilities. I remember a telegram about the Duo for violin and cello, asking, 'Is this glissando possible?'

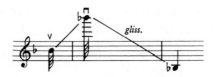

Ravel's house, 'Le Belvédère', at Montfort l'Amaury

and another demanding, 'Come quickly with your violin and the twenty-four Caprices by Paganini'.

It was the time when he was writing *Tzigane*, that violinists' minefield. He thought Paganini might be able to suggest to him some unsuspected obstacles, but I can safely say Ravel was the more devilish of the two! His subtlety went beyond the field of music. How many discussions we had about matching colours for ties, fancy handkerchieves and jackets! This New Year of 1938 is the first one for twenty years which has not (alas!) found me in a state of perplexity on the subject of Ravel's ties. We would have been discussing since October the three ties I used to give him at the start of every year: 'Now then,' he would say,' I've ordered two jackets, one beige and one violet-blue . . . What would you say to a red tie? Or perhaps an indigo one?'

Ravel was a friend. Once he had decided on an interpreter for the first performance of a new work, he was unmoved by pleas from the greatest star performers. 'Anyway,' he used to say, 'I prefer rehearsals to great names.'

Hélène Jourdan-Morhange
Maurice Ravel par quelques-uns de ses familiers (Paris, 1939), pp. 163–9

The garden at Montfort

When the weather was fine, Ravel used to receive his friends on the terrace behind his house and serve aperitifs and coffee. We must not forget his cocktail period, because he was a master barman! He used to stay downstairs for an eternity concocting his secret mixtures without suspecting that his poor visitor (who might well have come from Paris to show him some music) might have preferred his presence to the cocktail. Finally he would emerge from his cellar, carrying in triumph his latest brew, which he would name ironically 'Phi-Phi' or 'Valencia'.[1] It was often a curious mixture but his

---

[1] *Phi-Phi* was an operetta by Henri Christiné, first performed in Paris in November 1918 and several thousand times after that. 'Valencia' was a popular song of the 1920s (see p. 46).

admirers, with their minds still on music, would applaud as though at a successful first night and Ravel would be happy.

There was also the ritual 'tour round the garden', during which the guest would discover the terms of enthusiasm Ravel reserved for the things of nature. In his delight he seemed to be seeing for the first time the thousands of little blue flowers that made up his Japanese lawn, the dwarf trees, those 'unsuspected colossi', bordering the 'little paths', leading to a 'little fountain' with its 'little basin'; because one of his last acts of extravagance was to turn the plot in front of the house into a Japanese garden (elsewhere he owned a large orchard). Passionate though he was about his garden, he never turned his hand to gardening; I never saw him holding a spade or pruning his fruit trees. But he liked to set the colours of flowers against each other and send his gardener on quests for the rarest species: I can still see his favourite pansies, like large, blue eyes. The house was surrounded by them, and on the walls masses of white and purple roses stretched up to the balcony. It was worth seeing Ravel, who was always gallant with female visitors, tenderly picking a few tiny flowers, tying them clumsily into a minute bouquet and offering them with ceremony.

I remember one season when ant-lions settled in his garden. He studied their habits with unbelievable patience and, sitting on his heels, with his index finger outstretched, he would provide a detailed commentary on the tragedy unfolding below him:

'Now look! Do you see, they dig out these great funnel-shaped hollows in the sand, they bury themselves at the bottom and they hide there, with their great scythe-shaped jaws, waiting to kill the female ants; they capture other insects too by throwing sand over them, and when they've smothered them they eat them.'

He loved looking at birds, butterflies and squirrels, but his heart belonged to cats. A family of Siamese lived with him, whom he adored, torturing them with clumsy caresses from his nervous hands, with their double-jointed thumbs and rather square fingers. They gave him a lot of trouble: the male disappeared, the female died of a broken heart and the baby, my little godson Mouni, died of poison. Ravel often used to write me 'cat letters' and my friends would be amazed to read, at the bottom of a serious missive: 'I've passed your request on to Mouni; and I lick the end of your nose.'

Hélène Jourdan-Morhange
Ravel et nous (Geneva, 1945), pp. 24–5, 32–3

Ravel was a child: a child when he was pleased with a new suit and could show off his gloves in the latest fashion; a child when he shouted at the top of his voice to one of the friends who had come to meet his boat in New York, 'You must see the stunning ties I've brought!'

He took a great interest in New York, but life in America cut across his habits. He wrote to me from Los Angeles: 'I'm seeing some magnificent cities and some wonderful countryside, but triumphs are exhausting! In Los Angeles I've left people in the lurch . . . I was dying of hunger!' That is a very characteristic material detail. Ravel liked to comment on the present moment; he experienced it so intensely that it pushed more important considerations into second place.

When he came back from his American tour a group of us went to meet him: his brother Edouard, M. and Mme Bonnet, Maurice and Nelly Delage and Marcelle Gerar. As I gave him his bouquet, all done up in frilly paper, I said, 'Aren't we kind to come and meet you?' To which he replied indignantly: 'I would much rather you hadn't!'

Ravel was an uncompromising person and at his most demanding as a friend. One had to get used to his silences, to his phobia about writing letters, and not mind his temporary disappearances. He would often work for nights and days on end, spending weeks over a few pages, and then suddenly he would reappear and be his usual self, affectionate, restless and friendly. For all his air of an independent bachelor he was a creature of

The 'welcome home' party at the Le Havre quayside after the composer's American tour. From left to right, Maurice Delage, Marcelle Gerar, Hélène Jourdan-Morhange, Ravel, Nelly Delage and Edouard Ravel.

habit: nothing would have prevented him spending Christmas Eve with Paul Clemenceau and his family.[1] Even if he had not seen them all year, he would arrive, cheerful and surprised at their surprise.

Knowing his own weaknesses, Ravel used to shut himself up at Montfort when he wanted to work. He found it hard to resist the temptation of a friend or a telephone call summoning him to Paris for a concert or a rehearsal: always a good pretext to visit the city of lights, alive with the sounds of evening, jazz and the gossip of

---

[1] The brother of Georges Clemenceau, 'The Tiger'. Mme Paul Clemenceau was the dedicatee of 'Ronde', the third of Ravel's *Trois chansons* for mixed choir.

his young friends. Ravel adored Paris by night. 'Shall we go for a drink?' And, surrounded by young people, he would be off to 'Le Bœuf sur le Toit' or 'Le Grand Ecart', to revel in the decorations, the lights shaded with multi-coloured cellophane, the negroes, the saxophone and Clément Doucet at the piano.

He found enjoyment in everything. I remember one particularly gay evening – *L'Heure espagnole* was being revived at the Opéra and we were toasting its success with a few glasses of champagne. Finding the necessary euphoria to unbutton my admiration, I said emphatically: 'Ravel, you're a genius!' He burst out laughing and said, calling our friends as witnesses: 'She must be drunk to talk such nonsense!' For the rest of his life he was haunted by this joke; whenever I congratulated him with any warmth he would ask wryly: 'You're sure you're not drunk?'

His straightforwardness was proverbial. At the first festival of his music in the Salle Pleyel one of his admirers cried out, 'Bravo, Ravel, a triumph!' He replied, a shade ironically, 'Oh no, just the fashion!' He said things like that because he really believed them and always spoke of his music with serene detachment.

I find I see all these memories in perspective against those of his terrible last years . . . Ravel no longer able to read or write, spending hours on his balcony looking at his beloved view: a vast horizon, cleft by valleys, with a church near by. I can see him and hear him, already having difficulty finding words, telling me of Chabrier's tragic end. 'Horrible, isn't it?' he would say, 'to go to a performance of *Gwendoline*[1] and not recognize your own music!'

Ravel could recognize his music, but his was a worse tragedy. The last concerts he went to were a real torment. In July 1937, after Inghelbrecht and the Orchestre National had given a wonderful performance of *Daphnis et Chloé*, he took me by the arm, dragged me away from the crowd and in the car began to sob: 'There's so much

---

[1] Chabrier's only serious opera, first performed in Brussels on 10 April 1886.

music still in my head.' I tried to console him by saying his work was complete. He replied angrily: 'I've said nothing, I've still got it all to say.'

Ravel was very fond of his garden. He used to wax enthusiastic speaking about the soil, nature and animals. And indeed one had to admire his Japanese lawn made up of thousands of little blue flowers, his dwarf trees ('those unsuspected colossi') and all the strange plants which had gone towards 'japanizing' his garden. Ravel chose them meticulously, like his harmonies. His love of things Japanese corresponded to his taste for what was precious and perfect. There was even a tiny room in the house full of assorted Japanese objects; and he was delighted by his friends' astonishment when he proudly announced: 'All this . . . is fake!'

His house was governed by a family of Siamese cats who caused him any number of problems. His house-keeper, Mme Revelot, told me he was inconsolable when his little Mouni was deliberately poisoned. I remember the time when he was writing his Sonata for violin and piano and I often used to go and help him copy out parts and put in the bowings and fingerings. One, two, then three Siamese cats used to come prowling among the pages of manuscript, leaving their fivefold muddy foot-prints as an emblem of friendship. Ravel could discern, beyond their reserve and their pretended indifference, a faithful devotion which, perhaps, he likened to the noble, impenetrable pride of the Basques.

Only he could have written the cats' duet in *L'Enfant et les sortilèges* with such accurate onomatopoeia. One day we were singing this duet when the cat family, in some distress, walked into the room. I must add that Ravel's cat imitations were exceptionally good!

Hélène Jourdan-Morhange
ReM, Dec. 1938, pp. 193–7

Manuel ROSENTHAL

He was very proud of his Coleville apples and his Passe-crassanes pears and various other fruit that he grew and which he used to serve up very proudly when you had lunch with him. His gastronomic tastes – not really gastronomic, let's say culinary tastes – were extremely simple. He always had an enormous steak which he would eat rare, almost raw, with very few vegetables, he didn't like them. We would almost always start with mackerel in white wine, and he liked opening a jar of pickles. Then this steak and after that a piece of Gruyère. As you see, nothing out of the way for the cheese course. A fruit salad, or some fresh fruit from the garden, a pear or an apple. Always a very little drop of white wine. He never drank much wine, instead a regular Pernod before lunch and a cocktail before dinner. For years, these were his great pleasures in life.

Manuel Rosenthal
interview with Rémy Stricker, 'France Culture', 1985, quoted in Marcel Marnat, *Maurice Ravel* (Paris, 1986), p. 498

Valentine HUGO

Valentine Hugo (née Gross) was an artist and stage designer. She was a friend of Satie and, for a time, of Cocteau. She married Jean Hugo, the famous writer's great-grandson.

I remember a lunch arranged by Ravel and me at his house in Montfort l'Amaury in 1928 to which I was to bring Victoria Ocampo, a writer and director of the Buenos Aires literary review *Sur*. There were six of us at table and we chattered endlessly and tucked into an excellent meal. But suddenly I realized that Victoria was not really with us. What was the matter? On the way, in the car, she had seemed so happy. Firstly, the main dish had garlic in it, which she was not used to. But secondly, she had arrived at the composer's house, overflowing with admiration, ready to pay him lavish compliments about his music and, by the end of the meal, we had still not spoken about Ravel's music and, as friends of his, had no intention of doing so. We knew him: there were days when he did not want to talk about music and less still about his own.

After lunch we went and sat on the terrace, as Ravel liked to. It was raining a little but that did not stop us taking photographs while Ravel entertained us with his musical toys. We all had a good time but Victoria remained withdrawn and did not join in the fun. I found out the explanation ten years later when she wrote an article in *Sur* on the occasion of Ravel's death. Obviously she still loved his music, but the man himself had disappointed her. I had forgotten to warn her that Ravel did not like praise, as it were, directly pinned on to him like a decoration; or that his simple warmth was the greatest homage this purest of artists could have offered to a beautiful woman he did not know, alive with repressed enthusiasm, and whom he must have found extraordinarily intimidating.

Valentine Hugo
'Trois souvenirs sur Ravel', *ReM*, January 1952, pp. 142–3

Marcelle GERAR
(1891–1970)

Marcelle Gerar was a French soprano, who specialized in contemporary music. She recorded the song cycle *Shéhérazade* in 1929.

The Party at Montfort l'Amaury – 10 June 1928

The sculptor Léon Leyritz had met Ravel in my flat and was very keen to make a bust of him. I acted as go-between and the reply was, 'All right, as long as I don't have to pose . . .' Leyritz accepted the challenge, though Ravel did allow him to make some sketches while he was rehearsing his Violin Sonata. Shortly after, Leyritz told me, 'The bust is practically finished, but I would still like Ravel to come just once to my studio so I can make sure I haven't botched the proportions.'

'Well, write to him, or give him a ring . . .'

The reply was characteristic: 'I'll come tomorrow sometime between ten in the evening and three in the morning.' And he did, with a group of friends. Leyritz was happy to find the proportions were not botched and Ravel said, 'It's my best portrait!'

That was the year Ravel had his American triumph and I thought his friends would be happy to celebrate this double success. A surprise garden party was planned and, like all self-respecting surprise parties, the host was the first to be told about it so that he could oversee the invitations.

The party at Montfort l'Amaury. Ravel is seen in profile, pointing with his left hand, at second right behind the table

'My job,' Ravel said, 'will be to look after the cocktails, the wine and the *petits pois* out of the garden.'

On the appointed day guests arrived at Montfort by car and train and Leyritz brought the stone bust, whose positioning was the centrepiece of the occasion. Tables were set out on the terrace and though a few drops of rain did fall they were not enough to dilute the sauce of the *petits pois*. Someone began to sing, 'Petit Ravel, c'est aujourd'hui ta fête . . .' but stopped instantly as the *Maître*'s face began to tighten – he was always sensitive about his size. Meanwhile Honegger and Roland-Manuel acted as waiters, dressed in white aprons.

After lunch we played blind man's buff. Ravel was in a very gay, carefree mood, borrowed Mme Gil-Marchex's cloak and Hélène Jourdan-Morhange's hat and did a dance in drag. We then went off to Rambouillet to drink port and had dinner at Versailles. Ravel then took the hard core of the party to a cabaret and, through a deafening din of jazz, while the rest of us were beginning to droop, launched on a closely-reasoned discussion with Léon-Paul Fargue about the nature of Art, full of surprises and paradoxes, till four o'clock in the morning.

Marcelle Gerar
ReM, Dec. 1938, pp. 182, 183, 185

In October 1932, nine months after conducting the first performance of his G major Piano Concerto, Ravel was involved in a taxi accident in Paris and suffered cuts and bruises. Whether or not this had any permanent effect on his health, by the summer of 1933 he was having problems coordinating his movements. Long periods of rest produced no improvement and the solitude of Montfort began to be oppressive.

Hélène JOURDAN-MORHANGE

In spite of being tired, Ravel often came to Paris. His faithful housekeeper, Mme Revelot, who looked after him devotedly until his death, would put him on the bus at Montfort and one or other of his friends would meet him at the Porte Maillot. Then we would have a drink at the café on the corner and take him to his brother's place in Levallois[1] where Ravel had a room; not that he ever really moved into it, even when he was well, because his work always took him back to Montfort. Even so, he was always impatient to see it. A large bed-cum-divan, set into a light wooden frame, doubled up as a bookcase while the woodwork round the wall turned itself into a bar! This was something he had promised himself long ago; there must be a bar in the room with two or three high stools with the right sort of feet, the cocktail shaker, some large glasses and a multiplicity of drinks.

Needless to say this bar was never used and the great housewarming party we planned remained an unrealized project. It was the project and its mystery that Ravel loved. The realization, even of a party, made him anxious: there were letters to write, invitations to send, one had to be sure of *being there* on a precise date, glasses had to be bought, etc. A little ante-room gave access to the main one. Ravel did it up with nickel furniture like a dentist's, and with circular rugs which looked as though they had been cut out of steel. Very ingeniously, he had masked the view of the chimneys in Levallois with little concave window panes (from Austria, I think) which completely distorted the perspective. The sight of the factory chimneys thus became anything his imagination wanted to make it. Ravel was always aware of fashion and had a certain predilection for surrealism, but he never wanted to examine the profound reasoning of the young men who intended to change the universe – he simply found in this new language material for his reveries.

---

[1] Levallois-Perret is a north-western suburb of Paris.

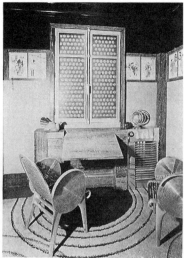

Ravel's rooms in his brother's house at Levallois-Perret. *Left*, the bar and the bed which gave the composer the impression that he was sleeping under a bridge. *Right*, the window with distorting panes and the armchairs which were made in an aircraft factory

But Ravel's room could not come to life without the poet who saw such beauty in it. As the reality of life became more distressing, 'the work of art' became less part of him; and so his only consolation was to be with nature and in his beloved forest of Rambouillet.

Hélène Jourdan-Morhange
Ravel et nous (Geneva, 1945), pp. 247–9

XI

As friend and companion

Désiré-Emile INGHELBRECHT
(1880–1965)

Désiré-Emile Inghelbrecht was born in Paris and began his conducting career there in 1908. He was a friend of Debussy and in 1931
founded the French National Radio Orchestra, which he ruled with
a rod of iron. In the early years of the century he was one of the
'Apaches'.

I remember Ravel searching for a musical phrase which
would serve as a rallying call for our little group.
Orchestral players all over the world had long since
adopted the first four notes of Beethoven's Fifth, so there
could be no question of using that. We thought first of a
theme from Rimsky's *Sheherazade*, but its chromaticism
and leaps of a fourth were not ideal for the open air
performances we had in mind. After much hesitation and
discussion Ravel decided on the opening of Borodin's
Second Symphony (although *Pelléas* was then all the
rage, Russian music was no less so).

We took it in turn to play host, but there was nothing
of a mutual admiration society about our meetings. Ravel
was the organizer and, although he certainly did not
refuse to have his music played and replayed, he was
more interested in performances of other people's music.
At that period practically the only Russian music played
in the major concerts was Borodin's *In the Steppes of
Central Asia* and Tchaikovsky's 'Pathétique'. But the
whole orchestral repertory was published in the form of
piano duets and that was a time when every painter and
doctor had learnt to play the piano; so there was no
shortage of duet teams to play in shifts all through the
evening.

We were therefore well prepared for Diaghilev's arrival from Russia, and Ravel was an obvious choice to compose *Daphnis*, in which one can at times detect traces of the Slav music he had done so much to make popular.

Désiré-Emile Inghelbrecht
ReM, Dec. 1938, pp. 119, 120

All accounts agree that Ravel, when on form, was highly stimulating company:

Emile VUILLERMOZ

Although Ravel was born in the far south he had no accent. His voice was slightly muted, gentle and hesitant, as far from being precipitate as it was from being a drawl. But he had a characteristic way of letting his voice fall slightly at the ends of phrases; it was, if you like, his form of ironical punctuation. When he delivered himself of one of those perfectly fashioned ideas which were his speciality, he would make a very characteristic gesture: slipping the back of his right hand quickly behind him, he would do a sort of ironical pirouette, lower his eyelids to conceal the mischievous twinkle, and end his little speech abruptly with a falling fourth or fifth. You can find these inflections everywhere in the *Histoires naturelles* and in *L'Heure espagnole*.

Emile Vuillermoz
Maurice Ravel par quelques-uns de ses familiers (Paris, 1939), pp. 59–60

ROLAND-MANUEL

In 1911 Ravel was living near the Etoile at 4 avenue Carnot. As Satie and I were about to go through the entrance to the apartment block a small man appeared whom I took at first to be a jockey. He was wearing a bowler hat and an elegant raglan overcoat. A malacca cane with a curved handle hung on his forearm and, when I was introduced, the enthusiasm of my handshake sent his cane flying through the air and when we rushed to pick it up we all bumped into one another and burst out laughing. To start with, Ravel was usually reserved and polite, but this incident broke the ice. In the years that followed I often noticed in him this ability to be amused by nothing much: an ability common to children and great intellects.

He shared the apartment on the avenue Carnot with his mother, a charming woman whose sensitive face was surrounded by a halo of white hair, and his brother, whom he complained of never seeing: Edouard Ravel was an engineer who got up early and, Maurice being a nightbird, the two met only on the stairs. From the window of the apartment you could see the Arc de Triomphe. On the walls, which were covered in watered silk, was a fine portrait of Ravel's father by Marcelin Desboutin, a gouache by Paul Sordes and two Japanese prints. There was nothing to indicate to a visitor that a composer lived there. Ravel the magician liked to keep even the apparatus of his tricks hidden, and it was only rarely that a pencil or a piece of manuscript paper was left on the table or on the piano, which was almost always shut. The only score I sometimes saw on the music-rest was the Breitkopf edition of Sixty Sonatas by Domenico Scarlatti and the only manuscript, some years later, was of Maurice Delage's *Poèmes hindous*, covered with fearsome arabesques in green ink.

Ravel had a way of greeting newcomers which could be disconcerting: a mixture of coldness without arrogance,

which could seem affected, and the utter simplicity and
naïvety of a child. However great his liking for you,
however close his friendship, the tone of his greeting
barely changed. Added to which, he was always incapable
of adjusting the expression of his courtesy to the age and
standing of the person he was addressing, with the result
that the young felt much more at home with him than
people of importance, who were considerably surprised to
find themselves accorded no special status. We, his friends,
were grateful to him for his direct, sincere manner,
as we were for a frankness free of all condescension.

Ravel did not regard friendship as a contract for the
distribution of praise, and in the course of the master–
pupil relationship which we soon adopted his frankness
sometimes took on a tone of asperity. Today I can bless
this harshness, but more than once I found it hard to
take. He would encourage me, as a consolation, to make
an analysis of works which, old-fashioned as they were,
stood in my eyes as the abomination of desolation; for
example, he gave me as a model the dream of Des Grieux
from *Manon*. Suggestions like this were a scourge to my
tiro's vanity. I tried to bring our disagreement into the
open by quoting instances from his own works, but he
was quick to point out that his boldest ideas were
grounded in reason and shaped in the classical mould,
and that I was mistaking means for ends; beautiful
harmonies had no autonomous existence, their charm
resulting from a chord in the right place or from a
modulation which simultaneously surprised the ear and
fulfilled its expectations. So I learnt to recognize that
Daphnis was a '*lied* in five sections' and that there was no
chord in my beloved *Valses nobles* that could not be
justified in the textbooks of Reber and Dubois. Truthful
as he was, he did not feel the need to parade his *sincerity*
before the world. The confusions produced by the abuse
of this word irritated him visibly and he was delighted by
some words on the subject I discovered in a preface
written by Remy de Gourmont: 'Sincerity is barely an
explanation: it is never an excuse.'

In any discussion of the discrepancies in the allotment of talent to mankind he would shrug his shoulders: 'Everybody's talented; I'm no more so than anyone else. With a little application each one of you could do what I do.'

If it is true that all art involves imitation, then no artist believed the dictum more than Ravel did. Both to Maurice Delage and to myself he expounded the principle that a composer had only to place himself in front of a master-piece like a copyist in the Louvre in front of a Titian or, to be less severe, a landscape painter in front of a clump of trees. He never tired of saying that one must not be afraid of continual imitation: 'If you have nothing to say, you cannot do better, while waiting for the ultimate silence, than repeat what has been well said. If you do have something to say, that something will never be more clearly seen than in your unwitting infidelity to the model.' He was quite happy therefore to compare his Trio with the First Trio of Saint-Saëns and his *Valses* with those by Schubert from which he had borrowed the epithets 'noble' and 'sentimental'.

He simply could not understand that an artist might tap other resources than those of his *métier*. One day I told him I was convinced I had to *start* by knowing my *métier* and he enquired with heavy irony what I intended to do the rest of the time, adding that one had to start by learning the *métier* of others and that a lifetime was not enough to perfect one's own.

His general culture, which was exquisite without being particularly broad, had given him exactly the right materials to suit his aesthetic, providing Baudelaire as his friend and counsellor and, through Baudelaire, Edgar Allan Poe – the Poe of *The Poetic Principle* and *The Philosophy of Composition*. How many times have I heard him recite his Baudelairean catechism: 'To create an archetype, that is genius' or 'Inspiration is merely the reward for working every day'!

The Ravel we knew corresponded in almost every detail with Baudelaire's definition of the dandy: an elegant coldness, discreet refinement in dress, a horror of triviality, a refusal to grant a government the right to decorate one . . . to which we might add a taste for company, without troubling to hide his contempt for it except to stand firm against the stupid remarks of the snobs. Sociability may have been a natural need for him but effusive expressions of camaraderie went very much against the grain: apart from his family and his student friends Ricardo Viñes, Marcel Chadeigne and Charles Levadé, Ravel addressed no one as 'tu'.

The idea of sacrificing or undertaking anything at all in the interests of his career, indeed the idea of his having a career as a composer, never entered his head. He was never rich and did not expect to be so. His ignorance about money was on a par with his lack of interest in it and his pupils can testify that they could never repay him for his lessons except by gratitude, which he would not even allow them to put into words.

Above all – and this was the ultimate in dandyism – Ravel was supremely detached from his own work. I can still see him, on 8 June 1912, arriving late for the first performance of *Daphnis et Chloé* by the Ballets Russes. We could not find him in the auditorium of the Châtelet Theatre so we went hunting up and down the corridors. The three knocks announcing the start had already been sounded when we saw him arriving in his gala outfit, holding under his arm a long package done up in brown paper. As we were pressing him to take his place, he asked very deliberately which box Misia Sert[1] was in. 'Haven't you got a box?' I asked. 'Yes,' he said, 'but I want to give Misia Sert something.' And while Nijinsky was making his stage entrance with his herd of goats, Ravel opened the package and presented Mme Sert with a magnificent Chinese doll.

Roland-Manuel
Maurice Ravel par quelques-uns de ses familiers (Paris, 1939), pp. 142–8

---

[1] See p. 19.

Alexandre BENOIS
(1870–1960)

Alexandre Benois was a Russian painter. He took part in preliminary discussions about *Daphnis et Chloé* and designed both the costumes and the décor for *Boléro*.

Ravel, a magnificent composer and a charming man, was an ardent admirer of our performances and dreamed of creating a ballet with me. We had not finally agreed on the subject, but it was decided in principle that the action was to take place in Spain. Ravel had a genuine cult for Spain, which I shared. We did not hurry ourselves. We had the whole summer in front of us and decided to spend it together at Saint-Jean-de-Luz, situated half a mile from Ravel's native place Ciboure. Every day we met on the *plage* and went for long walks together.

In those days Ravel was very gay and fanciful. I remember particularly one occasion during the last days of that happy summer, when dear Maurice, behaving like a mischievous schoolboy, flew in a wide circle and at terrific speed over our heads on a huge merry-go-round at the Ciboure Fair, shouting abrupt greetings to us every time he went past.

Alexandre Benois
Reminiscences of the Russian Ballet (London, 1941), pp. 365–6

Alma MAHLER
(1879–1964)

Alma Mahler (née Schindler) married Gustav Mahler in 1902. She continued to hold an important place in Viennese musical life after his death in 1911. Ravel stayed with her in October 1920.

Alma Mahler and her daughter, Anna

Among my musical house guests in those years were Alfredo Casella and Maurice Ravel. Casella came only for Ravel's concert . . . but Ravel stayed alone with me in my little flat for three weeks. He even used the place for concert rehearsals.

As a guest he was remarkably interesting. Food was still so scarce in that early post-war period that we mostly ate our frugal meals by ourselves, and I had occasion to study him at leisure. He was a narcissist. He came to breakfast rouged and perfumed, and he loved the bright satin robes that he wore in the morning. He related all things to his bodily and facial charms. Though short, he was so well-proportioned, with such elegance and such elastic mobility of figure, that he seemed quite beautiful . . . During Ravel's stay in Vienna I induced him to accompany me to a Schoenberg concert – it was the Chamber Symphony, if I am not mistaken. Ravel was very nervous throughout the performance. 'No,' he said when we got up at the end, 'that isn't music; that comes out of a laboratory!'

Alma Mahler Werfel
And the Bridge is Love (London, 1959), pp. 147–8

Hélène JOURDAN-MORHANGE

After the concert I saw coming towards me, mumbling to himself quietly, a slim, precise, nervous little man with greying hair, whose sparkling eyes and pointed nose reminded me of a good-looking fox: it was Maurice Ravel. He gave an official bow and ceremoniously kissed my hand. He said nothing about our interpretation of the Trio, but lavished all his praise on the cellist Delgrange and the splendid piano playing of Robert Schmitz. I thought my own playing had displeased him and I was glad he did not hold it against me. A few minutes later Delgrange came rushing towards me in a huff:

'I must say, your friend Ravel is charming! For ten minutes all he would talk about was your tone and how good Schmitz was.'

Schmitz likewise had heard no praise except of his two colleagues . . .

Thus, at my first meeting, I discovered Ravel's emotional *pudeur*.

Weeks and months often went by without Ravel giving any sign of life. Then he would reappear, welcoming as ever and amazed at your amazement. Externals of behaviour mattered not at all to him and I have often seen him be warmer towards total strangers than to his close friends; the latter knew his heart, he used to say, and did not need to be reassured by words. Frequently 'pushy' admirers had more chance of seeing him than his own circle. I remember one young man and his friend who did not leave Ravel alone for more than six months. They went to collect him at Montfort, took him out to dinner in Paris, and followed him when he went to nightclubs and to see his friends. Then one day Ravel asked me point-blank, 'What's the name of that young man who's always with me?'

Among his best friends were Maurice Delage and his wife Nelly.

'They're a true pair,' he used to say admiringly, 'they're never apart for a moment. If I had a wife she would have to be like that with me . . .'

Then, after a few seconds' thought, he added confidentially: '. . . but I'd never stand it!'

Was it a need for independence? Did he really want a mate?

'My mother's seen it all,' he would explain. 'I go for a walk and forget to come back . . . and I find her desperate. And as I'm a bad-tempered man, when I'm the one who's at home I'm very fussy about having my meals on time.'

Hélène Jourdan-Morhange
Ravel et nous (Geneva, 1945), pp. 18, 20–1, 23

Henri SAUGUET
(born 1901)

Henri Sauguet was born in Bordeaux and came to Paris on Milhaud's advice. He studied with Charles Koechlin and was a member of the 'School of Arcueil', founded under Satie's aegis. He was elected a member of the French Institute in 1976.

Just after I had arrived in Paris in 1922, I met Ravel one day in the street. He was walking up and down and stopping to gaze at length in the shop windows. He was dressed with a rather affected elegance and I was particularly struck by the colour of his hat. Then he went into a bookshop. I followed him in and found myself hunting through the same box of second-hand books. Suddenly our hands touched and I heard him say, 'I'm sorry! Have you already chosen this book?' I then spoke a fatal word: 'No, *Maître*, it's yours if you want it.'

I saw his face contract with annoyance. He left the shop looking irritated and a little further down the street took a taxi.

Henri Sauguet
ReM, Jan.–Feb. 1939, p. 12

Léon-Paul FARGUE

Ravel took part in our walks through Paris, in our café reunions, our enthusiasms and our crazes. Like us, he attended every last performance of *Pelléas*, loved Mallarmé, Marcel Schwob,[1] the tenth *arrondissement*, the old gates of Les Halles, exhibitions of precious objects, heavy black tobacco weighed out on scales made of horn, merry-go-rounds, the Eiffel Tower, the little theatres of Belleville and the stately ladies of the night who understood nothing about anything . . .

---

[1] Marcel Schwob (1867–1905) was an essayist and critic with a particular interest in the language and period of Villon. He was fluent in both English and German.

Ravel practised his own brand of dry humour. I see him still, like a debonair wizard, ensconced in his corner of 'Le Grand Ecart' or 'Le Bœuf sur le Toit', telling me endless little stories which had the same richness, elegance and clarity as his compositions. He brought off an anecdote as he did a waltz or an adagio.

Léon-Paul Fargue
Maurice Ravel par quelques-uns de ses familiers (Paris, 1939), pp. 158–60

In the following reminiscence, by André Beucler, who came to Paris from the provinces in the early 1920s, Ravel and Fargue are in conversation. Fargue speaks first:

'I've got an idea for a ballet. As a matter of fact, I've told you about it at least a dozen times already. All these *cafés chantants*, these tunes whistled in the streets, these birds you hear warbling in the voices of the pretty girls – they're the violins of Paris. Do you see what I mean?'

'You mean that certain aspects of this town which people love so madly, or certain interpretations of it, could be made to play in a ballet the same role as the violins in an orchestra.'

'The idea is there exactly as it comes to me. I'd never attempted to dot the i's and cross the t's. The chief thing is that it must be true, bursting with life, a beautiful counter-blast to despair. Wouldn't you, too, like to translate that everyday magic which lies in popular songs? A sort of immense anonymous letter from the street, giving us its message of love. Do you remember? . . . It wasn't so long ago that people used to go to concerts as today they go to football matches. But you turned your backs on melody and they stayed away. It's as though the be-all and end-all was to look down the wrong end of the telescope. You no longer dare do anything, you no longer want to, on the pretext that it has been done already. It's as though present-day music was, above all, anxious to gain time. While the true aim of music is to waste it!'

'Do you think so?' Ravel asked pensively.

'I'm sure of it . . . And I should like to start straightway, posting myself at some street corner to collect material for my ballet . . . But I must take you one day to my quarter – Faubourg Saint-Martin, Boulevard de Strasbourg. That's the real place for songs. We could concoct the thing as we wandered about.'

Ravel was lighting a cigarette. It must have been at least the tenth since we'd joined him in the restaurant. Suddenly he turned on Fargue to ask:

'By the way, why did we arrange to meet this evening? Didn't one of us want to discuss something?'

'Yes. But which of us was it? And what was it we were to discuss?'

Neither could remember. It wasn't merely mutual affection that had brought them together that night. There had been something else, and in groping for it they rummaged far back in their memories. Walking beside them in the dawn, I was at times able to follow, at others completely lost. At one moment they had got on to a luncheon party given heaven knows how many years before in honour of Galliéni, who, it seems, resembled Léon Blum. A minute later they were arguing about fashion. According to the composer, fashion in music was created by music itself. It was not, as in painting or literature, an external influence which could lead the art astray. Finally they returned to the ballet, *Les Violons de Paris*, and decided the idea was worth looking into.

Dim lights had already been lit in the bakers' shops. Now it was the turn of the dairies to open. Little by little the streets were peopled by those who work by day and sleep by night – postmen, busmen, greengrocers. From here and there came the clatter of a dustbin lid.

Maurice Ravel hailed a taxi that was crawling up the Rue Fontaine. Before leaving us he said to Fargue:

'When are you coming to Montfort?'

'At this moment it's both too near and too far.'

'You know the house, don't you?'

'Le Belvédère? I should think so! I've spent the night there.'

Ravel turned towards me.

'Bring him along with you.'

I was still blushing when the taxi disappeared from view. Fargue asked me what I was going to do. I answered that I was going straight home to write down all I'd heard that night.

But I wasn't to get away as easily as that.

'It's not a bad idea,' he said, 'but your hotel doesn't attract me. And you'll understand what I'm getting at when I tell you that this is just the time of day when human solidarity is most acceptable. Besides, I must explain Ravel to you before we part. He's not nearly so serene a person as you might think. He's wracked by all sorts of little internal pangs and tortured by the itch for perfection. No artist has ever been harder to please. Nothing leaves his hand till he has perfected it. He sometimes reminds me of Leonardo da Vinci or of the fringes of a wave drawn by Hokusai . . . Do you know, he was turned down three times for the Prix de Rome. Not that he was really keen to have it, of course, but he felt there were intrigues going on. Then there was that business with Debussy over the *Sites auriculaires*. He's above that sort of thing. For he's a grand man, and, what's more, it's been given to him to bring colour back into French music. Sometimes I may seem to speak lightly of him, but don't be misled by that. I admire him enormously . . . At first he was taken for a impressionist. For a while he encountered opposition. Not a lot, and not for long. And, once he got started, what production! . . . Of course, you know he's got a heart of gold. We'll go and see him in his home one day; though first of all I intend to drag him round a bit . . . To come back to his work, he's an engraver, if you like, a very delicate engraver, but he holds his burin in a grip of iron. I can't think of anyone else for my *Violons de Paris*. Can you?'

It was broad daylight now. A bright morning, fresh, but with a promise of heat to come. We wandered on, feeling that there was nothing better to do than to watch the birth of a Paris day.

A few days later Fargue launched a little 'season' of his own in a café in the Place Clichy. It lasted a good week, and during that time the poet, one might say, 'held *salon*'. For that's what it really amounted to. It was all arranged over the telephone, and he and I would be the first to arrive, to secure places 'on the sea front' as Fargue put it. Sometimes the *salon* was held before dinner, sometimes after, as was most convenient for our guests.

The most faithful members of our group, whose emblem was *Les Violons de Paris*, were Ravel, Ricardo Viñes, Sem[1], René Kerdyk, René Guillère, and Gignoux. Others came occasionally – Giraudoux,[2] Duvernois, and Poiret,[3] for whom I had already acted as lecturer and master of ceremonies at a dress show given by him in barges on the Seine. He was delighted by the idea of the ballet and only too ready to undertake its wardrobe. Giraudoux, who was constantly travelling, explained at great length one day that songs were the only sort of Esperanto which had ever succeeded. Sem and Duvernois maintained that nothing would ever come of the idea unless Fargue set to and wrote a libretto for it.

But L.P.F. preferred to sit back and relax, as though already exhausted by an arduous day's work. He preferred to toy with the idea, to bask, like those around him, in the contemplation of what it might be, surrendering himself to the luxurious idleness of the moment, listening to the raucous sounds of the street blended with the airs played by the café orchestra – ballads, snatches from operas or films – which Ravel, smiling and serious at the same time, indulgently dubbed one evening *la belle musique de terrasse*. Beautiful it was with the beauty of the moment, played to a handful of restless, dissatisfied sensibilities, to whom it was all part of the bustle around and the traffic before them and the drifting clouds above.

On another evening Ravel was telling us that popular

---

[1] Sem, the artist and cartoonist.
[2] Jean Giraudoux, the novelist, playwright and diplomat.
[3] Paul Poiret, the fashion designer.

songs were a direct expression of popular thought, and
were inspired by a desire to wreak vengeance on the office
and workshop, from which they were an escape. It was
Ricardo Viñes who added that they were also an instinc-
tive expression of hope. We had, of course, returned once
again to *Les Violons de Paris*, and we one and all urged
Fargue to get something written to embody the idea,
even if it were no more than twenty lines of verse.

But he was too slippery for us; we could never pin him
down. There was still a lot of preliminary research work
to be done. He wanted Ravel to come with him and
explore the field. They ought to spend an afternoon, for
instance, in the *Passage de l'Industrie*, which was, so to
speak, the headquarters of French song. True enough!
Passage de l'Industrie was certainly a misnomer. It
ought rather to have been called *Passage des Compositeurs
et Editeurs de Musique*. Here undoubtedly was the
centre of *Paris qui chante*, though since then the world of
song has partially migrated to other quarters.

In the end Ravel was won over, and a few days later we
found him, at the precise time arranged, gazing into the
window of a music shop in the Boulevard de Strasbourg.
Sometimes a customer inside would have a gramophone
record played over to him before deciding to purchase it.
Sometimes one would hum a tune, as the only way of
specifying what he wanted. And Ravel gazed and listened
with an intensity of interest that was a pleasure to watch.
He was discovering something, or at any rate seeing
something familiar in a new guise. I am reminded of
what Roland-Manuel said about him in a broadcast
twenty years later:

Our great musicians have never been ashamed of admiring a
pretty tune from a *café concert*. It is said that it was in
watching ice-cream vendors dancing a fandango at Saint-Jean-
de-Luz that Ravel picked up the first theme of his Trio in A, a
theme which he believed to be Basque, but wasn't.

He was more smartly dressed than usual that day. His
appearance was somehow distant, as though he had
dropped down into another world. He was like the

passenger on a liner who goes ashore for an hour or two
on some strange island. Soon the ship's siren would
sound and the enchantment be broken. We walked up to
him. He started, then smiled. He thanked us for having
brought him there. Then, without any transition, he
complained of the gulf which existed between the music
of most of the songs and the words.

'The music's full of ingenious finds. It's fascinating.
There are lots of phrases I'd like to have written myself.
But the words! The words! . . . And yet I'm forced to
admit they couldn't have been different. Without them,
all these melodies would be lost; perhaps even they'd
never have been invented . . . It's a good thing men have
remained troubadours to this day. For there's no getting
away from it – there's an old tradition there, a faith. It
has its rules; it has its style. There's more to it than just
saying fatuously: "I love you".'

For a moment or two he mused. He lit a cigarette.
Then he went on:

'What we're listening to here, my dear Léon-Paul, is
not really popular song at all – not popular in the sense of
universal. It's the *chanson de Paris*. That is to say, it's
already in itself a symphonic derivative. It's a product of
virtuosity and *savoir-faire*. In other words, there's a style
of song which is essentially Parisian, just as there are
Basque songs or Neapolitan, Russian or Provençal. It's a
sort of folklore . . . So your *Violons de Paris* exist all
right. And the bards . . .'

He pointed to the photographs in the shop window.
Yvonne George, Mistinguett, Paulus, Bérard, Chevalier,
Georgel, Damia, Mayol . . .[1]

Caught up in the game, he came with us to half a dozen
other places, particularly those bazaars which are sometimes called *Galeries de la gaîté française*. Finally he
declared gravely:

'*Mon cher maître et ami*, I am entirely at your disposal.
Whenever you want to start work, my house at Montfort
l'Amaury is open to you.'

---

[1] The most famous popular singers of the time.

Alas! Fargue had, or pretended to have, something else to do in the neighbourhood – his own special quarter. He dragged us round to the Town Hall of the 'Tenth', where in the end he forgot all about us. And that was the end of *Les Violons de Paris,* at all events as far as he was concerned.

Many months later we came upon the composer of *Boléro* again in a friend's house. He was improvising at the piano, and no sooner did he catch sight of Fargue than he started developing a bit of a sentimental song which was then the rage. With remorseless logic he played with the theme, turning it over, juggling with it. Suddenly he stopped and turned round.

'That's called,' he said, and hesitated, as though to keep secret a moment longer his title for the ballet which had gone down the drain, 'that's called *Folklore.*'

Fargue instantly plunged into a long and dithyrambic explanation of *Boléro* to a lady at his side, who must have been somewhat puzzled by the contrast between his eager speech and his roving eye.

'It's a stunt which has the grandeur of a *Magnificat* and the discipline of an antiphon. It's perpetual motion concealed in music, which, by the way, is its proper place. We needed it. It's irreplaceable. It's a Columbus's egg of instrumentation. It's a dive into the mysterious heart of monotony, into the depths of universal rhythm. It's a . . . '

He might have gone on for a long time reciting this *Miserere*, but Ravel mercifully came over to deliver him from his remorse. And to prove the sinner was forgiven, he took us that very evening to dine in the little restaurant in the Rue Fontaine where we had met that night which had witnessed the birth of *Les Violons de Paris*.

André Beucler
Poet of Paris, Twenty Years with Léon-Paul Fargue, tr. Geoffrey Sainsbury (London, 1955), pp. 58–66

Princesse Edmond de POLIGNAC (1865–1943)

The Princesse de Polignac was born Winnaretta Singer, of the American sewing-machine family. For forty years her salon was one of the most prestigious in Paris. Ravel dedicated to her his *Pavane pour une Infante défunte*.

A few years ago, when a concert was organized by my professional musical friends at the Salle Pleyel, and the programme comprised only works that had been written for or dedicated to me, Maurice Ravel was kind enough to conduct the orchestra when it played his *Pavane*. After the concert a few friends joined me and the Princesse Illinsky, who, I imagine, had never heard of him before, as she was not very interested in music. At one moment they seemed to be in very deep conversation, and when I asked, with some surprise, what could be the subject of their serious talk, Ravel turned and said 'Oh! we are talking about death' – an answer that surprised me, especially as they seemed in the highest spirits when they finished their discussion.

Princesse Edmond de Polignac
'Memoirs', *Horizon,* vol. 12, no. 68, Aug. 1945, pp. 127–8

XII

On tour

With Marguerite Long in Berlin, 1932

Marguerite LONG

When, in the midst of wildly enthusiastic ovations, Ravel seemed far away and had to be physically goaded to stand up and take a bow, it was not that he was indifferent to these expressions of admiration but that he was still listening attentively to his music. Anyone who knew him well could testify that his legendary absent-mindedness was in no way deliberate. Even if it sometimes had its ludicrous side, his good humour and sunny disposition allowed him to enjoy his own stupidity. He forgot his luggage, lost his rail ticket and his watch (these accidents occurred regularly on every journey), and kept not only his own post in his pocket but mine too, which sometimes had disastrous consequences. 'We're collecting memories,' I used to tell him, and we both laughed . . .

I remember one characteristic incident. One day in Prague Ravel wanted to find a particular kind of flask, made of a special crystal, to give to the mother of his pupil Roland-Manuel. Even though we had a concert that evening there was nothing for it but to comb the city from end to end! We came back totally exhausted but he was happy to have found what he wanted and to be able to take it back to the good lady, for whom he had an almost filial affection. Several months later, visiting him at his house, I saw the precious packet, unopened. He had forgotten to give it to her!

Forgetfulness of this sort did not mean that Ravel was uncaring. If he was reserved, secretive and distant with people who were pushy, he was the most reliable, discreet and faithful of friends. Because of his appearance, his witticisms and his love of paradox he often contributed to the legend of his own 'coldheartedness'. But despite appearances his was a sensitive and passionate nature, wounded by the least slight. He used to say, 'One doesn't have to open up one's chest to prove one has a heart.'

Marguerite Long
ReM, Dec. 1938, pp. 172, 173

Madeleine GREY

The first time I met him was at my first concert with an orchestra, the Pasdeloup, in 1921 under Rhené-Baton. I sang some classical arias and afterwards in the foyer I saw coming towards me a small, elegant man in a black and white check suit with a straw hat and a cane. He congratulated me in his usual warm, discreet manner and asked me if I would like to work at some of his songs, which would suit me perfectly. I asked his name but had no idea of the honour he was doing me as I knew his music only vaguely. Still, I accepted, saying, 'Monsieur, I'm always delighted to work at something new'. He immediately sent me the *Chants hébraïques* which bowled me over. As soon as I had learnt them, I went to sing them to him at Saint-Cloud, where he was then staying with his friends the Bonnets. He was pleased and, as I was leaving, presented me with a huge bouquet of white roses which he had picked in the garden.

On tour he was a delightful and amusing companion, almost anachronistically courteous. He always insisted on carrying my suitcase, which made a strange sight, the case being nearly as big as he was. His absent-mindedness was disconcerting, too: he would forget a concert or the time of a train! I remember one day at Lyons I was waiting for him on the platform. As the time got near there was no sign of him, so I ran up the stairs of the Hôtel Terminus four at a time and found Ravel contemplating an assortment of fancy handkerchieves, unable to decide which one went best with his suit. We would have missed the train that day if I had not begged the stationmaster to hold it for this famous traveller . . .

He always insisted on being perfectly turned out, with a pair of shoes to match every suit; which meant he always had piles of luggage. His famous trunk used to take up two-thirds of the luggage rack, which made already difficult journeys even more so. Our tour of Spain, for example! We visited a dozen towns in only a few weeks and the trains in 1929 were so slow you could almost keep up with them on foot. There were no couchettes either and the crazy timetables had us changing trains in the middle of the night. Ravel did not mind because he had always been an insomniac anyway and he talked non-stop. I was practically dead with exhaustion . . .

Happily, there were compensations. At every stop we were greeted like royalty with fanfares and wind bands. Banquets were given in Ravel's honour on a pantagruelian scale, with no less than thirty different dishes. My figure and my liver both suffered and I can see now the indignation on the face of a *maître d'hôtel* when I asked him, in the course of one such feast, to serve me some steamed fish! As for Ravel, he enjoyed it thoroughly, being a practised gastronome and a great lover of local cuisine. Occasionally he went too far. One day in Marseilles he was amazed at having a terrible attack of urticaria after consuming a veritable mountain of sea-urchins.

But apart from the triumphs there were also the disasters. At Malaga, for instance. The works we were performing went right over the heads of the audience, who were not used to modern music at all. So, in twos and threes, they began to tiptoe out of the hall. Even the President of the society which had invited us crept out in shame at the behaviour of his flock. So that when we came back on stage to acknowledge the applause, the auditorium was pretty well empty. Anyone but Ravel might have been cross; but he was quite without vanity and thought it was funny – he said it reminded him of Haydn's Farewell Symphony! 'Those poor people!' he said, 'they didn't understand any of it. Never mind, let's go for a walk.'

In Madrid the guests of the French ambassador behaved worse still. While I was waiting to sing, sitting in a corner trying to calm my nerves, Ravel started to play his Sonatina. But people went on talking as though nothing had happened. Ravel got flustered, lost his way and in his anxiety to get to the end went straight from the exposition of the first movement to the coda of the finale. The whole thing lasted no more than four or five minutes. But so little notice were they all taking that nobody realized and the piece was warmly applauded. When he came to collect me he was delighted with this bit of mystification and immediately lit up one of his usual cigarettes.

He smoked like a chimney and only the sort called 'caporal bleu'. On tour he always took a huge quantity with him in case they were unobtainable, and I can still hear him saying, 'Oh dear, here's Madeleine Grey, I'll have to go and smoke outside!' His friend Paul Valéry used to say Ravel's continual need for tobacco served to increase the smokescreen between him and the fools of this world.

He used to come to my apartment to rehearse and as soon as he arrived he often used to sit down at the piano and start playing Chabrier's *Chanson pour Jeanne* which he loved; and he would say, 'Why don't you sing it, it's so lovely?' He accompanied like a composer, that's to say well, but he did have his little foibles. For example in 'Aoua!', the second of the *Chansons madécasses*, which starts on a high, unprepared G, he used to say, 'I'll give you the note surreptitiously; I'll pretend to be rubbing a bit of dirt off the key like this . . .' and he did, at every concert.

Madeleine Grey
interview for *Le Guide musical* (never published, as the review went bankrupt; sent to the editor by Mme Grey)

XIII

Last years

With Jacques Février and Mme Jacques Meyer, 1937

In the summer of 1933 various alarming symptoms began to appear, affecting Ravel's coordination. Writing became difficult and he had to be careful not to put cigarettes into his mouth the wrong way round. Periods of rest and holidays abroad did nothing to stem the progress of the disease, which now prevented him from putting on paper the many musical ideas which were in his head.

Théophile ALAJOUANINE

Théophile Alajouanine was a well-known brain specialist whom Ravel's friends persuaded to examine him. The following extract comes from Alajouanine's Harveian lecture, given to the Harveian Society on 17 March 1948.

My second example is that of a famous musician whom I followed for over two years. He belonged to the pleasing class of musicians who have introduced a novel style, an original manner, and have expressed in a particular language a personality which will endure in the history of his art. At the peak of his artistic achievement, rich through an abundant and varied work, already classic, which expresses a delicate climate, Maurice Ravel is struck down by an aphasia.[1] His aphasia is of a complex nature: it is a Wernicke aphasia of moderate intensity, without any trace of paralysis, without hemianopia, but with an ideomotor apractic component. The cause, though indefinite, belongs to the group of cerebral atrophies, there being a bilateral ventricular enlargement; but it is quite different from Pick's disease. Oral and written language are diffusely impaired, but moderately so, without any noticeable intellectual weakening. Memory, judgment, affectivity, aesthetic taste do not show any impairment on repeated tests.

---

[1] An inability to express thoughts in words.

Understanding of language remains much better than oral or written abilities. Writing, especially, is very faulty, mainly due to apraxia.[1] Musical language is still more impaired, but not in a uniform manner. There is chiefly a quite remarkable discrepancy between a loss of musical expression (written or instrumental), and musical thinking, which is comparatively well preserved. With the help of two musicians, a favourite pupil of the master and a neurologist with great musical ability, we could study as precisely as possible musical tune recognition, note recognition (musical dictation), note reading and solfeggio piano playing, and dictated musical writing (copied or spontaneous). I apologize for giving such an analysis, but it seems to me essential in respect of the value of such a case-history.

Recognition of tunes played before our musician is generally good and prompt. He recognizes immediately most of the works he knew, and anyway he recognizes perfectly his own works. That recognition is not a vague one, for he is able to evaluate exactly rhythm and style as shown by the following facts. He immediately notices the slightest mistake in the playing; several parts of the *Tombeau de Couperin* were first correctly played, and then with minor errors (either as to notes or rhythm). He immediately protested and demanded a perfect accuracy. When playing the beginning of 'La Pavane de ma Mère l'Oye' which contains two exactly similar bars, one was omitted. The patient immediately stopped the pianist. He succeeded in explaining, in his halting speech, that the first bar was to link with the preceding part. The same is true for rhythm: if played too fast, he protests and has the music played again with its exact rhythm. Another remark: during these studies on musical interference of aphasia, my piano – because of the dampness of the winter – had become somewhat out of tune. The patient noticed it and demonstrated the dissonance by playing two notes one octave apart, thus showing again the preservation of sound recognition and valuation.

---

[1] An inability to manipulate objects.

On the contrary analytic recognition of notes, and musical dictation, are quite faulty, or seemingly so, since he could name only some notes hesitatingly and with difficulty. His numerous mistakes are due, very likely, to aphasia itself, and to the difficulty of finding the name of a note, a trouble exactly similar to name designation for common objects. The fact that reproduction of notes played on the piano, without giving their name, is quite good, seems to confirm this opinion.

Note reading is extremely difficult. From time to time a note is read exactly. Most often reading is impossible. The same is true for solfeggio. The trouble of name-finding may partly explain the failure. But there is something more, since piano playing is almost impossible after reading. A component due to apraxia supervenes therein. Anyway a quite definite discrepancy is noted between deciphering musical signs, and their visual recognition. If an analytic deciphering is almost impossible, on the contrary the patient is able to recognize at first glance whatever piece he has to find, and that without any error.

Piano playing is very difficult, since in addition to difficulty in reading, our aphasic patient has to search for the location of notes on the keyboard. He sometimes misplaces notes without being aware of it. For instance he plays the E-E instead of the C-C arpeggio, and plays it again and again, until his fingers are placed on the proper keys. He plays scales quite well, both major and minor ones. Sharps and flats are well marked. There is just a practical difficulty. He can play with only one hand (the right one) the beginning of *Ma Mère l'Oye*. With both hands he cannot decipher. He needs many exercises to play in that way. In spite of numerous exercises during a whole week he cannot succeed in playing the beginning of the 'Pavane' even with separate hands. On the contrary he has a greater performance ability when he plays by heart pieces of his own composition. He suddenly gives a right idea of the beginning of *Le Tombeau de Couperin* which is, however, too difficult to finish. Seven or eight bars are played almost perfectly, and he plays them, transposing down a third, without any error. When attempting an unknown piece he finds a much greater difficulty: he cannot play more than two or three notes of a piece by Scarlatti, which he did not previously know.

Musical writing is very difficult, although better preserved than plain writing. He writes dictated notes slowly and with numerous errors, but copying is almost impossible and requires from the patient enormous effort. On the contrary, writing by heart a portion of his 'Entretiens de la belle et la bête', though difficult and slow, is better performed than the other tests. Notes are better and more quickly placed, and he seems mainly disturbed by writing apraxia. Singing by heart is correctly performed for some of his works, but only if the first note or notes are given. He says that tunes come back quite easily, and that he can hear them singing 'in his head'. Musical thinking seems comparatively better preserved than musical language itself.

Though all artistic realization is forbidden to our musician, he can still listen to music, attend a concert, and express criticism on it or describe the musical pleasure he felt. His artistic sensibility does not seem to be in the least altered, nor his judgment, as his admiration for the romantic composer Weber shows, which he told me several times. He can also judge contemporary musical works.

Thus, in our musician, because of aphasia, and as already mentioned, because of a simultaneous apraxia, musical reading, piano playing, use of musical signs are much more impaired than expression and recognition of musical themes. Severe disturbance of realization, and difficulty of expressing a relatively preserved musical thinking, while affectivity and aesthetic sensibility are almost intact, are the main features of our composer's case-history. They explain why his work has been completely arrested by his cerebral affection.

Théophile Alajouanine
'Aphasia and Artistic Realization', *Brain*, 71/3 (Sept. 1948), pp. 232–4

Valentine HUGO

One afternoon in November 1933 Ravel's brother was going to bring him to my studio around four o'clock. André Breton and Paul Eluard had asked me to do everything I could to persuade Ravel to come to the offices of the review *Minotaure* on the rue Boétie so that Dr Lotte Wolff could take a print of his hands. They wanted to use the print, with those of other artists, to illustrate an article called 'Psychic Revelations of the Hand' which was to appear in the review at the beginning of 1934.

I knew that Ravel was suffering from some illness which had prevented him from working for several months, so I was not certain he would agree to come to Paris. But his brother told me he accepted with delight and asked if, on the day in question, he could bring Maurice to my studio and leave him with me for a couple of hours; at the end of that time Maurice would have to go on to the boulevard Delessert, and Edouard carefully gave me the address. He asked me not to keep him longer than two hours and not to forget the address Maurice had to go to, as he himself would probably not remember it.

About half-past three Ravel arrived, smiling, alert and happy. He was very taken by the bright studio looking out over the boulevard Clichy and wandered about looking at everything, enthusing over objects, some simple, some mysterious, which nowadays would be called 'surrealist'. Finally we sat down on a long sofa covered in red watered silk, which was the seat he liked best, and he began to talk about his operatic project on the subject of Delteil's *Jeanne d'Arc*.

Some time before he had asked Jean Hugo to do the décor and the costumes when his large work was put on at the Opéra. I myself was to be in charge of the making of the costumes, some of which he wanted to be very simple and some very sumptuous. He told me his outline, the captivating story of an extraordinary, innocent child of eighteen whose feet were firmly on the ground but whose head was lost in the heavens. And then suddenly he said:

'Valentine, I'll never write my *Jeanne d'Arc*. It's there in my head, I can hear it, but I'll never write it down, it's the end, I can't write my music down any more.' And he tried to explain, with a calm, terrifying despair, the fearful shadow which imprisoned all his ideas in his head.

I was overcome with pity, and to draw him out of the depression into which I could see him sinking I reminded him that we had a meeting at five o'clock. We took a taxi and in the cab he confided to me the emotion he felt at the prospect of meeting Breton and Eluard in a few minutes' time. He had been more passionately interested in the surrealist movement than he had let on and he would have liked to know the protagonists better. He said to me in a weary voice, 'Now it's too late'.

We arrived at the offices and Lotte Wolff carefully took Ravel's handprints, putting his hands first on a smoked plate, then on a piece of white paper. Now came the moment for Ravel to sign his name. When he was offered the pen he recoiled slightly and said, 'I can't sign, my brother will send you my signature tomorrow.' Paul Eluard said to me, much later when I recalled this awful moment, that he had the impression of Ravel, so far behaving easily and naturally if a little distant, suddenly becoming *frozen*.

Ravel turned to me and said, 'Valentine, let's go, now.' I can't remember saying goodbye, but we found ourselves at last out on the rue Boétie, holding each other by the arm. It was raining in torrents and night was coming on. Naturally, not a taxi to be had. Ravel's presence was normally so precise and tangible but now it seemed to be enveloped in isolating layers of damp muslin. I offered to take him where he had to go, but he said, 'No, Valentine, it'll be all right. They're waiting for me, they're used to it.' And he added gently, 'You can see me at the moment but shortly I'll look as though I don't see you any more and you'll feel as though you can no longer see me.'

We waited another quarter of an hour, I suppose, on the pavement opposite 25 rue Boétie; it seemed like a hundred years. Finally an empty cab appeared. I gave the driver the address and a lot of instructions. I said, 'Goodbye, Ravel', we embraced, I smiled at him, closed the door, the taxi drove off into the rain and disappeared. I walked slowly through the relentless downpour. As I went past a café I looked automatically at the time; it was half past six. We had far exceeded the two hours' grace.

I never saw Ravel again.

Valentine Hugo
'Trois souvenirs sur Ravel', *ReM*, January 1952, pp. 143–6

Eventually, in December 1937, his brother and various close friends decided it was worth risking an operation to try and restore Ravel to his true self.

Igor STRAVINSKY

I think Ravel knew when he went into the hospital for his last operation that he would go to sleep for the last time. He said to me: 'They can do what they want with my cranium as long as the ether works.' It didn't work, however, and the poor man felt the incision. I did not visit him in this hospital and my last view of him was in a funeral home. The top part of his skull was still bandaged. His final years were cruel, for he was gradually losing his memory and some of his co-ordinating powers, and, he was, of course, quite aware of it. Gogol died screaming and Diaghilev died laughing (and singing *La Bohème* which he loved genuinely and as much as any music), but Ravel died gradually. That is the worst.

Stravinsky
Conversations with Igor Stravinsky, Igor Stravinsky and Robert Craft (London, 1959), pp. 62–3

Ravel at first appeared to make a slight recovery, but he then relapsed and died in the early morning of 28 December 1937.

XIV

Two tributes

M. D. CALVOCORESSI
(1877–1944)

M. D. Calvocoressi, Greek by birth, French by education, was a writer and critic and another of the 'Apaches'. He was one of Ravel's earliest champions (Debussy waspishly dubbed him a 'valet de chambre') and Ravel dedicated to him 'Alborada del gracioso' from the *Miroirs*. After the First World War Calvocoressi moved to London, preferring to operate as a critic in a less venal atmosphere.

Ravel and I first met in 1898 or thereabouts at an 'At Home' to which I had been taken by a painter friend; and we frequently met there during a year or so. Our acquaintanceship – as later we confessed to one another – was marked from the first by reciprocal suspicion, because, although the hosts were altogether simple, worthy, and likeable people, their 'At Homes' used to be attended by quite a number of queer characters. Soon afterwards this suspicion became dislike: on his part because of the stupid remarks I used to pass on Debussy's music, on mine because of his sharp strictures on the music of Wagner, César Franck, and d'Indy.

Then, for a time, we lost sight of one another; but eventually we met again in the courtyard of the Conservatoire. He was still in Fauré's composition class, and I had obtained permission to attend Xavier Leroux' class of harmony for a time in order to rub up my technical knowledge; we started discussing music recently heard. The talk having veered round to Russian music, I suddenly asked him: 'Do you remember *Tamara* at the Concerts Lamoureux?' His eyes shone. 'Wasn't it lovely?' he replied. A few seconds later, to my surprise and delight, he burst out: 'Look here: I've got the piano-duet score. Let's meet and play it together.' I accepted eagerly. Poor Ravel! He little knew what he was letting himself in for. I was (and have remained) a vile bungler at the piano, and especially in duet playing. Anyhow, we met, and we played *Tamara* again and again, and after that a quantity of other Russian music. And in our love for this music we found a first common bond. By tacit agreement we ceased discussing Wagner, Franck, and d'Indy (having, I presume, given up one another as hopeless); and we soon became great friends.

He was generally considered a dangerous revolutionist and iconoclast, and absolutely disliked in official musical circles. His outspoken, but usually shrewd and well-weighed utterances on music old and new, many of them expressing views that may have been novel at the time, but are by now almost universally held, were bandied about in strangely distorted forms. I remember that one day Georges Marty (who was then a conductor at the Opéra and later became the conductor of the Concerts du Conservatoire) said to me: 'Oh yes! Ravel – he's the fellow who says that Beethoven couldn't score for nuts!' And Marty was a genuine, open-minded artist and man, who did not incline in the least to side with the enemies of progress, and who, had he been personally acquainted with Ravel, would soon have realized how far the gossip he happened to have heard in Conservatoire circles was from the truth. What Ravel would actually say and repeat, as I have often heard him do, was that Beethoven's scoring, especially as regarded the brass, was not always free from imperfections. But, as I have said, Ravel, at the Conservatoire, was a marked man, against whom all weapons were good.

He was then exactly as he is in the present year 1933, except that his hair was raven black and that he wore a beard. He carried out a good many experiments with that beard before deciding to do away with it for good and all. When first I knew him, he displayed a combination of moustache and short whiskers *à la* Franz-Josef. Then he tried a two-pointed beard, and later on a single-pointed. When one came into contact with him, the first impression was almost sure to be that of dryness and aloofness – very different from the semi-shy, semi-ironical reserve that was Debussy's first line of defence. He was endowed with a great capacity for indifference and also contempt,

On the banks of the River Nivelle, Basses-Pyrénées, at the time of *Jeux d'Eau*

but – as one found out quite soon – as great a capacity for admiration; and I was to realize, a little later, that behind the cutting manner, the irony, and the aloofness, there lurked an even greater capacity for affection.

He had matured early, both in temperament and in musical outlook. Indeed, he is one of the few composers of whom it may be said that their earliest works are thoroughly representative both in spirit and in idiom. He had a marked taste for the recondite, which people who did not know him well considered a sign of affectation. He was aware of this, but it did not worry him in the least. One day, however, he said to me, rather impatiently: *'Mais est-ce qu'il ne vient jamais à l'idée de ces gens-là que je peux être "artificiel" par nature?'*[1] And there can be no doubt that with this remark he defined one of his idiosyncrasies quite accurately – one that is, however, more apparent in his early works than in the later.

Many people alleged that the care he took to exclude from his music all that might resemble a direct expression of emotion was one of the signs of this artificiality. Once, in reply to a question of mine, he said that if he himself had to point out, in his music, passages in which the direct expression of emotion, far from being excluded, had been deliberately attempted, he would begin by selecting the opening of 'Asie' in *Shéhérazade*, then 'L'Indifférent' in the same set of songs, and, in the *Histoires naturelles,* 'Le Martin-pêcheur', and the end of 'Le Grillon'. He did not mention other obvious instances such as the slow movement of his String Quartet and the 'Oiseaux tristes' in *Miroirs*.

In his assessment of the music of other composers there was very little room for doubts, for half-hearted views, or even for any change of views. He may have learned, now and then, to like things which he had begun by not liking, but this must have occurred very seldom; and certainly he never came to dislike anything he had liked. His reasons for liking or disliking were definite,

---

[1] 'But doesn't it ever occur to those people that I can be "artificial" by nature?'

and for him final. To hear him pick to pieces a musical work, and then, by a swift process of reconstruction, deliver judgment, was an experience as instructive as it was fascinating.

His chief concern was with points of originality in idiom and texture. When calling attention to some beautiful thing, he would often wind up with: *'Et puis, vous savez, on n'avait jamais fait ça!'*[1] Questions of form seemed to preoccupy him far less. The one and only test of good form, he used to say, is continuity of interest. I do not remember his ever praising a work on account of its form. But, on the other hand, he was very sensitive to what he considered to be defective form. Once he gave rise to great indignation by declaring, in the course of an article, that Franck's form often was 'appallingly poor'.

I have just referred to the rare interest of his verbal comments on music. Curiously, when writing critical articles (which in later years he was often asked to do, but hardly ever did unless pressed) he either did not trouble, or remained unable, to recapture the lucid, subtle, and illuminating terms in which he accounted for his views when talking. Indeed, he sometimes tended to drive his points home with a bludgeon rather than with the rapier which anybody would have considered his natural weapon, and which he could, when he chose, wield skilfully and with devastating effects. In one article, he dismissed Beethoven's *Missa Solemnis* with the sole epithet: *'cette œuvre médiocre'*, leaving his readers to puzzle out his reasons for this unqualified verdict. Another time, he concluded a notice of d'Indy's *Fervaal* with the following remark: 'Even more significant than the composer intended it to be is the symbol of Fervaal, who, while proclaiming the victory of life and love, climbs the heights with the dead body of a woman in his arms.'

His dislike for much of d'Indy's music did not prevent his considering the *Symphonie sur un thème montagnard* a very fine work. There was little he admired in Wagner's

---

[1] 'No one had ever done that before, you know!'

music, but that little he admired very greatly. At a time when Gounod's music used to be sneered at in 'advanced' circles, he passionately called attention to the lovely things to be found in it. During the early years of our friendship, my impression was that he set no great store by the music of Saint-Saëns: the only two examples of it which he used to mention with praise were the symphonic poems *Phaëton* and *La Jeunesse d'Hercule*. But in 1910 or 1911 I began to notice, rather to my surprise (for the music of Saint-Saëns leaves me quite indifferent), that he was evincing great interest in it. And, indeed, signs of the influence which it eventually exercised upon him (a definite, although not very great one) are to be found in his Piano Trio of 1915, and in his Sonata for violin and cello of 1922.

On Russian music, he and I were in almost complete agreement. We gave pride of place to Mussorgsky, Borodin, and Balakirev. We loved Rimsky-Korsakov's music, especially his tone-poems and some of the early operas. We were not interested in Tchaikovsky, and we belonged to the number of the few who held Glazunov's early works in high esteem – especially his tone-poems *The Forest*, *Stenka Razin*, the *Oriental Rhapsody*, and the second and third symphonies. Of course, we were not blind to their derivative character: yet we felt that Glazunov displayed strong personality and fine imagination.

Another bond between us was our love of Liszt's music. We both felt very strongly on the matter, and were often driven to exasperation by the utterances of the people who were clear-sighted enough as regards the obvious defects of Liszt's music, but utterly incapable of seeing its obvious merits. The writing of a concert-notice gave Ravel the opportunity to refer to the matter in the following terms:

'It is to Liszt's defects that Wagner owes his turgescence, Strauss his churlish enthusiasms, Franck his ponderous ideality, the Russians the tinsel which occasionally mars their picturesqueness. But it is also to him that all these dissimilar composers owe the best of their qualities.'

He found little to admire in the music of Berlioz. He was extremely keen on that of Chabrier and Fauré; and he was, with Debussy, one of the very first to realize the interest of Satie's – it was he who gave me the idea of studying it at a time when hardly anybody knew it, and very little of it was published.

Soon after our friendship had begun to ripen, Ravel introduced me to his family. He was living, then, with his father, mother, and brother, in a small flat, Boulevard Péreire (those were lean times for all of us), and I became a frequent visitor to their home. He also introduced me to some of his friends, and soon afterwards a small informal circle of music-lovers was formed. We used to meet of an evening to read and discuss music. The reading was done at the piano chiefly by Ravel and Ricardo Viñes, but occasionally by other, less expert, players, the worst of whom was certainly myself.

To his intimate friends Ravel never grudged the pleasure of watching his new works grow. And, although he never invited comment, it was clear that he liked us to like his music. As a rule, we were responsive enough. Only once, in those early days, did a work of his bewilder us for a time. It was 'Oiseaux tristes', which he played to us again and again without our being able to understand what he was after. He was rather disconcerted to find us indifferent to a piece in which he had put so much of himself. Sordes summed up the humour of the situation by drawing a verbal picture of Ravel hawking about, on his extended finger, two forlorn little birds with whom nobody would have anything to do. But, after a while, we all learnt to love 'Oiseaux tristes'; and I, for one, cannot help wondering how I could have failed to enjoy it from the first.

When the set *Miroirs*, of which 'Oiseaux tristes' is part, was finished, Ravel inscribed one of its numbers to each of us: to Viñes, 'Oiseaux tristes', because, he said, 'it was fun to inscribe to a pianist a piece that was not in the least 'pianistic'; to Fargue, 'Noctuelles'; to Delage, 'La Vallée des cloches'; to Sordes, 'Une Barque sur l'océan'; and to me, the 'Alborada del Gracioso'.

His attitude towards criticism, favourable or unfavourable, was and has remained one of absolute, often contemptuous, indifference. Generally speaking, composers may be divided into two categories: those who declare themselves unaffected by criticism, and those who aver that they pay the greatest attention to it. But the majority of the former, even if they do not change their ways under the influence of anything that appears in print (and why indeed should they?) are now and then pleased, or hurt, or angered – which, after all, is only human; and an immense majority of the latter are either deluding themselves or – which is far more likely – offering a sop to Cerberus. Ravel, who has often proclaimed his indifference to criticism, is as good as his word: he may experience a natural pleasure in finding his friends (whether they be critics or not) responsive to his music, but the only opinions to which he ascribes a more general importance are those of the composers whose music he thinks well of. And, if I remember right, in his early days the only other critical judgments (quite apart from the question whether they referred to his own work or not) regarded by him as not altogether negligible were those which, belonging to what is usually described nowadays as the 'sensitized-plate' type (that is, not aiming at expressing anything but their writer's reactions), struck him as worthy of praise from the literary point of view.

He was, from the very outset, quite sure of himself, of his purpose, and of his technique. The one thing he cared to say about his music was that he knew exactly what he wanted to do, and why. One day he said to me: 'I may confidently aver that I never release a work until I am quite certain that I have done my utmost and could not in any way improve one single detail in it.'

The two facts that the Greek songs were Ravel's first venture in the harmonization of folk-tunes, and that one of his most important works is a ballet on a Greek subject, have given rise – though not very generally, it is true – to the idea that Greek subjects may have had some special attraction for him. There is absolutely no foundation for this idea. *Daphnis et Chloé*, like the Greek folk-songs, owes its existence to purely accidental circumstances, and Ravel did not think of the subject himself.

Besides, as soon as one begins to see him as he really is, it becomes almost impossible to think of him as capable of being attracted, for creative purposes, by anything not French. I am not referring, of course, to the influence exercised upon him by the rhythms and colours of Spanish music, which, like many other French composers, he was often tempted to use; nor to the mainly technical influence of Liszt, Balakirev, Rimsky-Korsakov, and Borodin. I am thinking of essentials – outlook and modes of thought and expression, character, and atmosphere: his 'Spanish' music, for instance, is as French as can be – and as French as Rimsky-Korsakov's or Glinka's 'Spanish' music is really Russian.

Ravel must be thought of as French first and last. At the time of which I am writing, he knew no single word of any language but French, though nowadays he can speak a few words of English, which he utters with a wonderful combination of the French and American accents. He had studied neither Greek nor Latin; all his acquaintance with the classics and with foreign authors he owed to French translations, and I am sure that often the French flavour conferred by these translations played a part in his enjoyment of them.

For instance, he had been, at an early date, greatly attracted by Gerhart Hauptmann's play, *The Sunken Bell*, and had started setting A. Ferdinand Hérold's French translation of it to music. Nothing of what he composed for it was ever written down, although he kept working at it, during many years, at irregular intervals, and used to play us excerpts which we liked very much. I have often wondered whether, knowing German, he would have been equally attracted by the original text; and indeed I remember his commenting lovingly upon the rhythm, colour, and musical quality of passages which were, of course, quite different from anything he would have found in the German.

As regards *Daphnis et Chloé*, he surely loved Amyot's delightful old French quite as much as the story itself. I also remember discussing with him the *Arabian Nights* and discovering to my amazement – simply because I felt otherwise – that, leaving aside the relative value, from the purely narrative point of view, of the French translations available, he far preferred Galland's eighteenth-century version, in which atmosphere, colours, and happenings are quaintly altered in accordance with French taste and habits, to modern translations such as that of Mardrus (then in course of publication) which attempted to preserve at least the illusion of a purely Eastern character.

More generally, he also loved the character that Greek, and likewise Chinese art, had acquired at the hands of their French imitators. When after the war he had taken, at Montfort l'Amaury, a house of his own, which he was able to furnish after his own heart, I had an amusing instance of this bent. He took my wife and me round the house, and while showing us one room exclaimed with glee: *'Voyez: ici, rien que du faux Grec!'* And then, as he opened another door : *'Et ici, rien que du faux Chinois!'*[1]

Exceptionally he once entertained the idea of learning Spanish, in order to be able to read *Don Quixote* in the original and to extract from it the libretto of an opera which he dreamt of writing. No translation, he said, and no librettist, could give him exactly what he wanted. But he never carried out this plan, and I have often thought how deplorable it was that he should have given it up. A *Don Quixote* from his pen would have been a work on a grand scale, certainly most racy and stimulating, and very probably true to the spirit of outward irony and latent compassionate tenderness which characterizes Cervantes' masterpiece – a spirit which no music inspired by it has to my knowledge ever succeeded in suggesting, even faintly.

---

[1] 'Look: here, nothing but fake Greek . . . And here, nothing but fake Chinese!'

But to revert to *Daphnis*. Ravel never thought of dealing with this particular subject in any form until 1909, when it was offered to him by Diaghilev, who, with the help of his advisers, had been eagerly casting round for subjects as well as for composers. Various libretti, all of them very conventional, had been outlined, and were submitted to Ravel to choose from. I well remember him, Diaghilev, Fokine, Bakst, Benois, and myself in Diaghilev's little sitting-room (red plush and mahogany, alas!) at the Hôtel de Hollande as it then was, finally deciding for *Daphnis* and offering suggestions as to particulars of plot and incidents, Fokine eventually casting the libretto into shape to Ravel's satisfaction.

I also remember that the very first bars of music which Ravel wrote were inspired by the memory of a wonderful leap sideways which Nijinsky (who was to be Daphnis) used to perform in a *pas seul* in *Le Pavillon d'Armide*, a ballet produced by Diaghilev that very season; and that they were intended to provide the opportunity for similar leaps – the pattern characterized by a run and a long pause, which runs through Daphnis's dance, pages 26 and after of the piano score.

I will add to this chapter one memory of Ravel, which has nothing to do with music, but which I think worth recording because it refers to one of the rare occasions on which I saw him lose his self-possession, and the only one on which I have known him display, publicly and actively, concern in, and sensitiveness to, purely human events outside the circle of the people he was individually interested in. I was not acquainted with him at the time of the famous Dreyfus affair; and it stands to reason that I am not referring to his activities and feelings when the war came.

It was after the passing of the death sentence on a French criminal named Liabeuf. Liabeuf, who was being constantly watched by the police because he was known as an anarchist, had been arrested for living on the earnings of prostitutes, and sentenced to imprisonment despite his protests of innocence. Released from prison, he had manufactured leather wristlets and shoulder-pads all covered with steel spikes, and, equipped with this formidable obstacle against arrest, had shot the two detectives responsible for his previous arrest and conviction. Several policemen were wounded before he was overpowered.

Hardly had the death sentence been passed than a petition was set afloat by a few people who, believing him to have been wrongly sentenced in the first place, considered that his revenge did not deserve capital punishment. Ravel was among the most eager to secure a reprieve. He would have liked me to sign the petition. He was, he told me, against the death penalty always. Quite apart from that, he averred that Liabeuf had been the victim of a trumped-up charge simply because he was an anarchist, and the blind fury which had led him to avenge his honour by shooting his accusers was understandable.

After Liabeuf's execution, Ravel was so upset that for a few days he shut himself up in his home, refusing to see anybody.

M. D. Calvocoressi
Musician's Gallery (London, 1933), pp. 46–8, 50–5, 66, 70–1, 77–81

ROLAND-MANUEL

To see Maurice Ravel for the first time was to be surprised at his diminutive height. After a short while it was no longer noticeable, presumably because his hard, spare, agile and slender body was so well proportioned that he appeared in perfect symmetry on a small scale.

After favouring side-whiskers in his youth, he enjoyed allowing his moustache to grow, and trimmed his beard, first to a point and later square. In 1910 he threw off the mask and became entirely clean-shaven, at last revealing his real features which were those of a Basque from the coast, with the dark complexion, hollow cheeks, and the

Ravel surrounded by pelota players at Ciboure, 1930

long nose common to the daring as well as the naïve type, brilliant, dark, and closely-set eyes, and thin lips, closed as if to hold back a secret. Bushy eyebrows; black hair, slightly curly, which began to grow grey after the forties, and became white and wavy after 1930. His whole appearance was both gay and enquiring, alert and smiling, the open frankness of his eyes giving the lie to the reserve of the firmly shut lips.

His slender and active hands were admirable for either pianist or conjurer, with their spare fingers and unusually curved thumb. His carriage was light and easy, and remained youthful in spite of the years. His lengthy stride betrayed his double mountain ancestry. His somewhat sombre and 'nasal' voice was inclined to be deep. If he ever had occasion to use his singing voice – which only happened under professional pressure – it still showed this so-called *blanche* delivery characteristic of the composer's spoken voice.

Ravel expressed himself very simply with the same spontaneous grace which appears in his letters. He spoke without any particular accent, like a well-bred Parisian. One single linguistic peculiarity betrayed his southern provincial origin; he constantly forgot to use '*si*' as an affirmative particle, and used '*oui*' when he wanted to contradict someone else's affirmation.

He never had the occasion nor perhaps the inclination to exercise and train his natural agility and physical skill. He was content to be an excellent swimmer and a tireless walker. His manual dexterity was very unequal: he was wonderful at modelling small objects with pieces of bread, but he performed the simplest actions clumsily and almost lazily. Here as elsewhere, he was alert and quick in difficult tasks only.

He was extremely fastidious about his appearance, and very obviously attentive to his dress, his ties, the cut of his clothes and the changes in fashion, an absorption which took the form of a most sober elegance which seemed to be unpremeditated.

A confirmed smoker, his 'caporal' tobacco was a more tyrannical urge than eating or drinking. It was rare for him to listen to a concert from beginning to end without sacrificing one or more pieces of the programme for a cigarette. It was owing to the remorse which sometimes followed such disappearances that Manuel Rosenthal became his pupil and one of his best friends. At one of the concerts of the *Société musicale indépendante*, which were mostly devoted to performances of works by unknown composers, Ravel slipped away during the playing of a Sonatina for two violins, to smoke what Léon-Paul Fargue used to call 'a life-saving cigarette'. When he came back we whispered to him that he had missed hearing a remarkable work. Like a child caught doing wrong, the master of *Daphnis et Chloé* went along to introduce himself to Manuel Rosenthal and to make his apologies, and invited him to come and see him. So began a great friendship.

Ravel's appetite was as sound as his digestion and in keeping with the general excellence of his health, which did not deteriorate till the end of his life. A healthy and discriminating eater, without overdoing his interest in food, he was yet the easiest of guests to satisfy when he used to come and take pot-luck. But offer him a good table and he was immediately the more inclined to be critical of it. His race showed itself in a liking for strong wines and spices which he himself called 'incendiaries'. In the ordinary way, however, he was very moderate in his tastes.

At a first meeting Ravel was courteous and reserved. His best friends could not help feeling secretly disappointed by the feeling that they were not able to become more fully intimate with him; for the most devoted sympathy and close relationship scarcely altered the manner of his greeting. It took a long time to discover that Ravel was the surest, most faithful and most profoundly affectionate of friends.

But the sort of affection he gave was virtually incapable of external expression, and only showed itself in unexpected acts and attentions. It seemed as if he felt uncontrollably awkward and almost physically incapable of putting his emotions into words. In short, he was a most sociable person – but the least communicative.

His desire for company, which was one of his fundamental needs, was only equalled by his horror of appearing as the famous man, of being exposed to the curiosity of worldlings and snobs, and having to attempt heartiness with men of position, who inevitably took little time in finding him out as a natural enemy of the Best People.

Ravel was, besides, incapable of adjusting his manners to the social rank of the person talking to him. Unskilled as he was in the art of being nobly bored, he would not have hesitated to turn his back on an Excellency in order to go off and play, like the child he was, with the children of the household.

For Ravel had never left the 'green paradise of childhood affections'. Genius for him was not Baudelaire's rediscovered childhood, but a childhood which was conserved, ennobled and communicated. At once both objective and credulous in outlook, nothing ever tarnished his pure and simple attitude to the world. The violence of passion and the tyranny of primitive instincts never obscured for him that ingenuous disinterestedness which assures the artist his freedom and guides him without swerving to the fundamental nature of things, leaving him free to absorb whatever he will.

Unlike those contemporary extremists of sincerity who get hold of the wrong end of the stick by being childish in their technique and cunning in spirit, Ravel instead uses cunning in his technique and keeps his spirit childlike.

He loved toys, minute knick-knacks, dwarf trees, and all manner of oddities, and convinced of their incomparable beauty, he either made everybody admire them at great length or he gave them as presents alike to grown-ups as to the children of his friends. Edouard Ravel had to spend several days in a nursing-home after an operation. With an air of infinite secrecy, his brother Maurice placed on his bedside table a little mechanical game of pelota, exquisitely put together.

His return from a journey to Venice was marked by presents to all his lady friends of baroque buckles in exquisite filigree work. I can still hear one of them exclaim as she opened her parcel: 'Heavens, how ugly, but how kind of Ravel!' But Ravel possessed the daring which belongs to the forerunners of fashion, and it was not long before this elegant lady was prominently wearing his gift.

Ravel possessed in the highest degree the tyrannical and teasing character of the spoilt child. His friendship, like his music, made lavish use of anticipation and surprise. But it was exacting and admitted no excuses.

Incapable of envy and indifferent to the idea of being its object, he never answered, even by contempt, the kind of hatred which in any human group attaches itself to those different from the rest. He was only jealous in friendship; but there he confessed himself to be terribly so. He found it hard to admit that he could be abandoned for anyone else. And as time did not count at all where he was concerned, he could not understand that it could count for his friends. For he did not allow a dependence on the clock, and with cunning virtuosity developed a genius for wasting his own time and making others waste theirs. On the other hand, no-one returned affection more generously – not in words, certainly, which he could not express; but by delicate attentions and secretly rendered services. For just as he wanted everything about him to take place 'as if it were a miracle', as Léon Leyritz has said, he himself took pains only to give pleasure by surprise.

Ravel was never heard to slander anybody. As for what he considered to be good in you, and the feelings you aroused in him, he waited for you to turn your back before he would give them expression. This reserve and frigidity which normally characterized him only really left him in the company of children, young women or kittens, whose company he equally enjoyed. The incongruity of this association must be forgiven, in so far as it brings us to the 'jardin féerique' of *Ma Mère l'Oye*, to the 'green paradise of childhood loves', where desires are not accompanied by remorse; where creatures are only loved for the beauty which they reflect; and where Péguy's[1] Holy Innocents play catch with their haloes.

'Naturally artificial': in one sense child, in another dandy. Both existed simultaneously in Ravel. He could almost be described in the same words Baudelaire used for the bearing of a man of absolute genius who 'had in him much of the dandy' and who 'indulged with pleasure in the most material vanities of dandyism . . . He had the same apparent coldness,' said Baudelaire, 'the same icy cloak, hiding a reticent sensibility . . . Beneath the same show of egoism he had the same devotion to his secret friends and to the ideas of his choice . . . One of his supreme preoccupations was, I think to conceal the turbulence of his heart and not to appear as a man of genius . . .'

A common and secret attachment to dandyism alone can explain why the same description can with equal justice fit two artists and two men so different in other respects as were Eugène Delacroix and Maurice Ravel.

---

[1] Charles Péguy was a Catholic writer, socialist and patriot, killed on the Marne in 1914.

Above all, and this is supremely the mark of the dandy, Ravel seemed to be completely detached from his own work. His music only interested him as something to do – to do well. Once the work was finished, and the game over, he planned another exercise. It was all very well to listen to others' music with the hope, always too far off, of the 'life-saving cigarette'; but his own was always too much for him – he used to flee.

The mention of 'game' brings us back to childhood – his true native land, the place of aimless yet ordered activity. The rule of the game, implying submission to the object, and the obstacle to be overcome – or to be created – were, and were to remain, the essential preoccupations of Ravel as craftsman. And when the final result, which motivates the form, does not spring from the arbitrary imposition of restraints, Ravel has to make use of creative imitation.

'Before I write a work,' Satie used to say, 'I wander round and round it with only myself for company.' Ravel's perambulations were endless. His work took shape very slowly but was usually given final form fairly quickly.

A walk was the invariable preliminary for setting to work. Long expeditions in the woods, whatever the weather: nightly walks across Paris, which sometimes extended to the Bois de Boulogne and beyond. After a concert or dinner in town, he often persuaded several friends to visit one of the cafés in the Place du Havre, and then go on to the Bœuf sur le toit or the Grand Ecart. When he set out once more, on foot, for a destination unknown even to himself, it would often happen that an exhausted companion would be curtly dismissed, so that Ravel might pursue alone, with his lengthy stride, his indefatigable noctambulism.

But these wanderings had sudden ends. He would shut himself up and generally without hesitation produce a definitive manuscript, which was instantly seized by the printers. He composed in the greatest secret. Here again everything had to be done – or seem to be done – by a miracle. His piano and his study table bore no trace of his work and gave no evidence of preliminary drafts. Nothing in the hands or the pockets: the conjurer juggled away even the apparatus of his tricks. Things were accomplished as though the piano-keys manipulated the printers' dies at a distance.

Although no one ever saw him composing, he let us watch him orchestrating as much as we liked. When thus engaged, he always had to hand Widor's *Technique de l'orchestre moderne* – an aid to memory which gave a list of trills and passages which could be played on every instrument. He also freely consulted the miniature scores of Saint-Saëns' concertos for piano and orchestra and the symphonic poems of Richard Strauss.

When he was orchestrating, he continually went from the table to the piano, so that he could hear the parts of an instrumental group to better advantage by separating them out at the piano. According to him, he composed as much at the piano as at the table, claiming that for him the chief use of the piano was for orchestration.

Although for him the professional discipline was the Thesean thread 'to guide the mind in the maze of Art', Ravel talked about it but little, and did not willingly enter into details of composition. Those young composers who used often to bring him their attempts and ask his advice, returned charmed by the simplicity of their reception and a little surprised by the severity of his uncompromising orthodoxy. 'The truth of it is, you don't know anything. You must work.'

Some of these phrases appear again, with the persistence of a 'leitmotif', in conversations he had with his disciples, who in chronological order were Maurice Delage, the author of the present book, and Manuel Rosenthal. I believe that they appeared equally often in his discussions with the composers whom he voluntarily helped out of his experience and his kindly sympathy, particularly Vaughan Williams, Maurice Fouret, Nicolas Obouhow, Louis Durey, Germaine Tailleferre, Lennox Berkeley and many others.

He loved Mozart with all his soul. He was devoted to Weber – 'the great romantic' – to Liszt, Chopin, Bellini and the Russians, with an obvious preference, though not a conspicuous one, for Borodin. Of the moderns, his admiration went first and foremost to Chabrier, whom he linked with Manet with the same feeling of affection. He did not understand how the composer of the *Roi malgré lui* could be taxed with vulgarity: 'How can this composer be vulgar when even two bars of his give away the author?' He considered Charles Gounod a forerunner of genius; and, in spite of the slovenliness of some of his writing, he did not hesitate to parallel *Mireille* and *L'Arlésienne*, insisting how much the latter owed to the former. Although by temperament and taste he was opposed to the aesthetic of Bayreuth, he had never wanted to share in those anti-Wagnerian frenzies which were the fashion in his day. In his youth he had been charmed by the fairy aspects of the *Ring*; in later years he came to regard Wagner 'primarily for what he was throughout – a magnificent musician'. As for Berlioz, whose genius was at the opposite pole to his own, he praised his daring, which he considered lacked merely the elements of a technique possessed by more mediocre talents.

His liking for Saint-Saëns' music showed itself especially towards the end of his second period – about 1910. His *Phaëton*, *Le Rouet d'Omphale*, and his piano concertos and chamber music showed him to be a great creator of values in the strict sense as applied to musical structure.

No pen can be expected to transmit the delightful spontaneity which lay at the heart of this little man of iron, who never truly revealed himself except to his intimate friends, and then not by effusions of which I have shown him to be incapable, but by sudden, unexpected confessions which manifested a candour and consciousness of self free alike from vanity and falsity.

He said one day to Maurice and Nelly Delage: 'It's lucky I've managed to write music, because I know perfectly well I should never have been able to do anything else . . .'

And to us, after the first performance of a contemporary work: 'He can take liberties I would not allow myself, because he's less of a musician than I am.'

To make a brief summary, the man was frank rather than eloquent; polite rather than cordial; with more sociability and vivacity than unselfconsciousness; with more devotion to friendship than indulgence in friendliness; and more sheer cleverness than all the rest put together.

Roland-Manuel
Maurice Ravel, tr. Cynthia Jolly, (London, 1947), pp. 127–36
(French edition *A la gloire de Ravel* published in Paris, 1938)

Index